C000183662
Dear Maria,
Thank you for all of your help with this book – it would all be rubbish without you! ♥ Dana xxx

the new WEST COUNTRY COOK BOOK

DILIGENCE PUBLISHING

FORD
6610

for Maria, Charlie and Jack xxx

Photography, styling, art direction and illustration by
David Griffen

Editor	Jane Griffiths
Editorial assistant	Maria Griffen
Additional copywriting	Rebecca Ritson
Recipe proofreader	Portia Spooner
Proofreaders	Louise Cole
	Rosie Smith
	Abigail Bruce

The fonts used within the book are:
Bickham Script, Gill Sans and Intro Inline

Printed and bound in China

ISBN 978-0-9576238-0-4

First published in 2013 by Diligence Publishing

CONTENTS

INTRODUCTION by David Griffen

I take pictures of great food.

It's a privilege that has fed not only an appetite to celebrate the chefs who create the dishes, but also to applaud the region that supplies the source of their inspiration: the South West.

Since relocating from Australia to the West Country almost ten years ago, I have been lucky enough to witness the stellar nature of the region's culinary development and capture the moments when produce, place and talent unite.

By the end of this book, you'll have seen the West Country through my eyes: travelled with me on a fishing boat to pull in mackerel and crab at dawn; got your boots muddy tracking down Dexter cattle with cliff-top views of the Celtic Sea; gone underground to sample cave-aged cheese; and shaken hands with fellow West Country food champions, the chefs themselves.

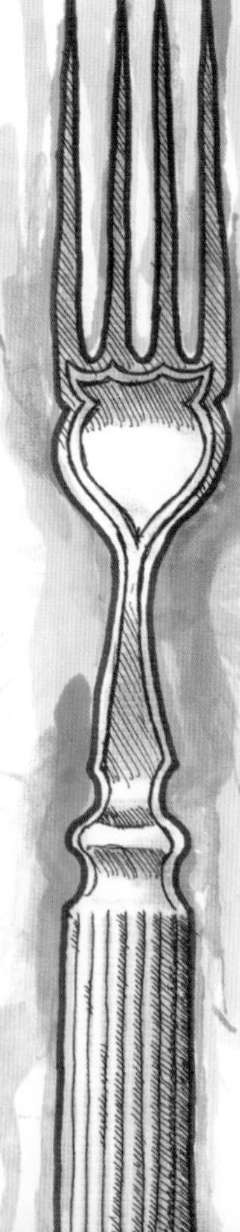

Working together, we've brought a shared passion to this project - pairing my images with their dishes in celebration of the new look, feel and, most importantly, taste of the region's invigorated food culture.

But new doesn't have to be complicated: clever cooking can be simple cooking. Focusing on key ingredients that can be found or foraged locally, the best of the region's chefs have come up with some lovely recipes which emphasise, rather than manipulate, the flavours of food in a uniquely West Country style.

Whether because the region's food scene has, on occasion, been dismissed as provincial, pasties or simply Padstow, or because of its geographical isolation, there's a special camaraderie amongst the community of cooks in the South West. This book is testament to this collective spirit.

I'm excited to share these recipes with you, inspire some tasty meals in your own kitchen and maybe even motivate you to take me at my word and come down and try the food first hand – the fact is that the galaxy of Michelin stars on show in this 'New South West' is merely a part of a larger universe of talented chefs lighting up the West Country.

This book, then, is a showcase: not of the top names in the business, although it has them; not of expensive or extraordinary ingredients – as the South West can grow, rear or catch them all; but, more, a celebration of the simple beauty and – let's be honest – fantastic taste of the best ingredients artfully combined.

Tasty stuff indeed!

"The attraction of Cornwall was always a special one for me and my family - so it made perfect sense to end up back here with my own family and business. And while I spend a lot of time travelling up to London on the train, when I come back across 'the border' (River Tamar), it really feels like I am coming home. "

"This Cornish rarebit mixture can also be spread over white fish fillets before grilling or baking to form a delicious coating. Sharp's is our local brewery and, in my opinion, a pioneer in the way it brews its beer. Sharp's Doom Bar has a lovely subtleness to it, making it perfect for cooking as well as being very easy to drink!"

CORNISH RAREBIT
with Doom Bar Beer

SERVES 4
PREP: 15 mins
COOKING: a few mins under the grill

120g	mature Cheddar cheese
60ml	Doom Bar beer
30g	plain flour
30g	breadcrumbs
1 tbsp	English mustard
3	egg yolks
1	loaf of bread *uncut*

Grate the cheese and place in a saucepan with the beer.
Heat over a medium flame until the cheese has melted and the mixture begins to bubble.
Stir in the flour, breadcrumbs and mustard.
Continue to cook gently until the mixture comes away from the saucepan cleanly and forms a soft ball.
It is important to keep stirring.
Remove from the heat and cool.
Beat in the egg yolks until the mixture is smooth and all the yolk is incorporated.
Slice the loaf into 'doorsteps'.
Lightly toast the 'doorsteps' under the grill on both sides.
Spread liberally with the Cornish rarebit mixture.
Place under a hot grill until the rarebit bubbles.
Cut and serve immediately.

CORNISH BLUE CHEESE

"To retain the beautiful green colour of this soup, try blending the recipe in smaller batches."

WATERCRESS SOUP
with Cornish Blue Cheese

SERVES 4
PREP: 15 mins
COOKING: 25-30 mins

For the Soup

3 large bunches of watercress
leaves removed and washed
1 large potato
peeled and thinly sliced
2 cloves of garlic
finely sliced
1 small onion
peeled and sliced
1L vegetable stock

For the Dressing

1 clove of garlic
peeled and crushed to a paste
1 tsp English mustard
sea salt and black pepper
2 tsp cider vinegar
100ml rapeseed oil
200g Cornish Blue cheese
broken up into small pieces

For the Soup

Heat a saucepan and add a little oil.
Place the onion and the garlic into the pan and gently cook for 1 minute - do not colour.
Add the sliced potato and cover with vegetable stock.
Simmer until the potato is cooked and then transfer to a food processor.
Place a frying pan on the heat and add a little oil.
Put the watercress in the frying pan and quickly fry and wilt.
Add the wilted watercress to the soup base in the food processor.
Blend for 3 minutes or until smooth.
Taste and add salt accordingly.
If the soup is not being served straight away, chill over ice to retain the green colour and place in the fridge until required.

For the Dressing

Whisk everything together apart from the oil and cheese.
Slowly whisk in the oil forming an emulsion.
Taste and season if required.
Add the cheese.

To Serve

Heat the soup until hot and pour into 4 warmed bowls.
Finish with the cheese dressing and serve.

FRESH GARDEN MINT

RED MULLET

RED MULLET
with Coriander, Mint and Anchovies

SERVES 4
PREP: 15-20 mins
COOKING: 3 mins

For the Dressing

10	anchovy fillets in oil
50g	coriander leaves
50g	mint leaves
200ml	rapeseed oil
25ml	lime juice
	sea salt to taste

For the Fish

2	whole red mullet (approx 500g each) *scaled, filleted, pin-boned and trimmed*
30	anchovy fillets in oil
1	lemon *zested*
1	garlic clove *finely chopped*
1 tsp	chopped parsley
	rapeseed oil to drizzle

For the Dressing
Place the 10 anchovy fillets, coriander and mint in a food processor and blend for 1 minute.
Add the oil and lime juice and a touch of salt and blend for 1 more minute.

For the Fish
Preheat grill to the highest setting.
Place the 30 anchovy fillets into a container and sprinkle over the garlic, zest and parsley.
Drizzle with a little rapeseed oil.

To cook the fish, place the red mullet fillets onto a grill tray and drizzle with oil. Season with salt and pepper and place under the grill.
Cook for 3 minutes until golden.

Serve immediately with the anchovies, dressing and a little salad.

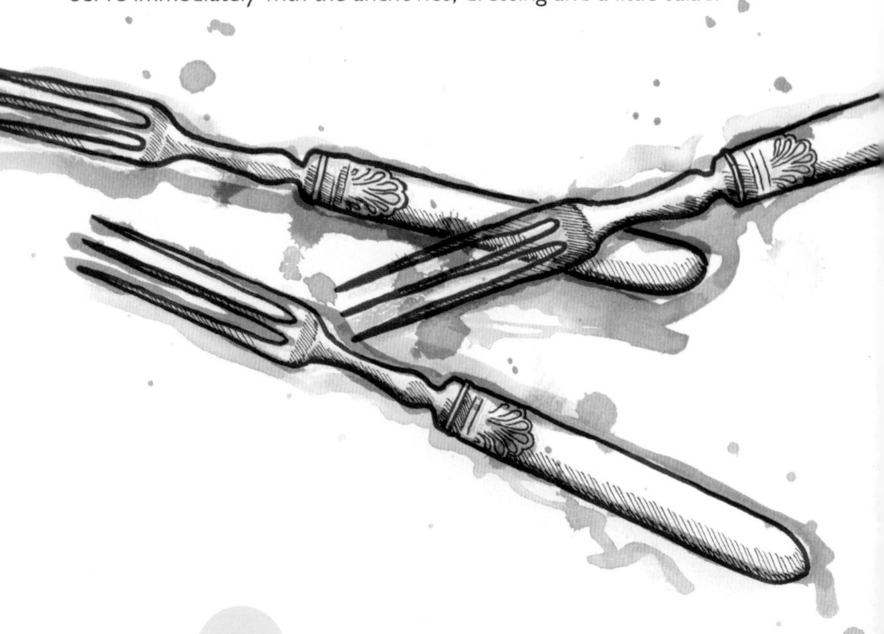

"The combination of eggs and smoked fish in the dish is a match made in heaven. It is simple to prepare and perfect to eat at any time of day; not just for breakfast. This recipe can also be made as individual servings using 4 small ovenproof omelette pans. Just share the mixture equally between the 4 pans and reduce cooking time to 2-3 minutes. This recipe is courtesy of Chris, head chef at my restaurant in Rock."

SMOKED MACKEREL OMELETTE
with a St Endellion Brie Glaze

SERVES 4 as a starter
PREP: 15 mins
COOKING: 10 mins

For the Brie Glaze

300g	St Endellion Brie
450ml	double cream
	creamed horseradish to taste

For the Omelette

4	large free-range eggs
2	large smoked mackerel fillets *flaked*
2 tbsp	chopped dill
4 tsp	cream
50g	butter

For the Brie Glaze
Cut the rind from the Brie with a knife, then dice the cheese.
Place the cheese and double cream in a small, heavy-based pan.
Stir constantly over a medium heat until the ingredients are combined and smooth.
Add creamed horseradish to taste and stir thoroughly.
Set aside until needed.

For the Omelette
Break the eggs into a bowl and beat together with the cream until well combined.
Put the butter in an ovenproof frying pan.
Place over a medium heat until the butter melts and begins to bubble.
Pour the egg mixture into the frying pan and cook gently for 4-5 minutes, drawing the mixture from the edges towards the centre until it is beginning to set.
Sprinkle over a spoonful of the mackerel pieces and the dill.
Stir through the egg mixture and continue to cook until the omelette is just set.

To finish
Spoon the Brie mixture over the omelette.
Glaze with a blowtorch or place under a preheated, hot grill until it turns golden.
Cut into 4 wedges and serve immediately.

PZ 30

BRILL

"When you are lucky enough to get the freshest fish on your doorstep, eating seafood raw is something you can do without worry. Brill, in particular, has a very good structure and a certain tenderness that makes it ideal either for eating raw or curing."

RAW BRILL WITH TARRAGON *and Orange*

SERVES 6
PREP: 15 mins

1kg	very fresh brill fillet *skinned and washed*
1	orange *peeled and segmented*
20	large tarragon leaves
100ml	extra virgin rapeseed oil
	sea salt to season

Slice the brill as thinly as possible and share it equally between the 6 plates.
Season with sea salt.
Slice the orange into small pieces.
Slice the tarragon into strips.
Divide the orange and tarragon equally over the plates.
Drizzle with rapeseed oil.

Serve at room temperature.

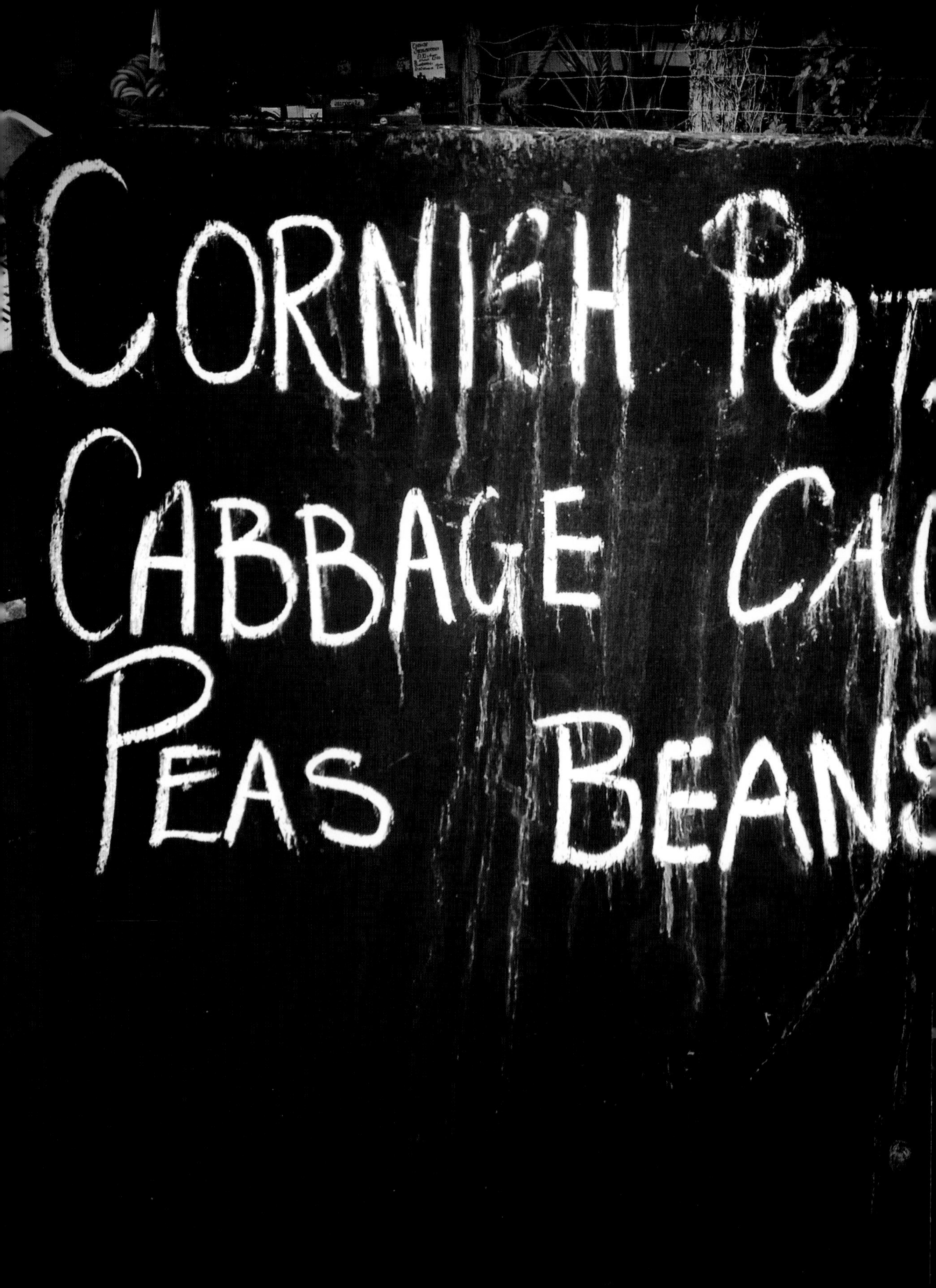

CORNISH
CABBAGE
PEAS BEANS

PETE BIGGS

"Working in Cornwall has completely opened my eyes to the fantastic produce this region has to offer. The county has the highest-quality fish, lobsters, crabs, mussels and oysters – not to mention the brilliant cheeses, asparagus and clotted cream. The beer is not bad either! "

I ♥ TEA

SMOKED MACKEREL

"Doom Bar beer (Sharp's brewery) adds a great flavour to the bread and fills the kitchen with an incredible smell when baking."

SMOKED MACKEREL, BACON & DUCK EGG
on Doom Bar Bread

SERVES 4
PREP: 30 mins
COOKING: 30 mins

For the Bread – makes 2 loaves

200g	light malthouse bread flour
300g	white bread flour
300ml	Doom Bar beer
35g	fresh yeast (or 14g instant)
10g	butter
20g	salt

For the Salad

8	rashers of cooked bacon *sliced*
4	duck eggs
200g	watercress leaves
2	fillets of smoked mackerel

For the Mustard Dressing

½ tsp	finely chopped shallot
½ tsp	English mustard
1 tsp	cider vinegar
100ml	rapeseed oil

For the Bread
Mix together all the ingredients, except the salt, to form a dough.
Knead on a lightly floured surface for 5 minutes.
Add the salt and knead for a further 2 minutes.
Place the dough in a bowl.
Cover in cling film and leave in a warm place until the dough doubles in size.
Remove the dough and roll into shape for 2 loaf tins.
Place in the tins and cover with a damp cloth.
Leave in a warm place for a further 45 minutes.
Preheat oven to 235°C.
Remove cloth, dust with flour and add a splash of water to create some steam and give a crusty finish.
Bake for 20 minutes.

For the Salad
Flake the smoked mackerel into large pieces.
Mix together the mackerel flakes, bacon and watercress.

For the Mustard Dressing
Combine the mustard dressing ingredients together and drizzle over the salad.

To Serve
Toast 4 slices of the Doom Bar bread.
Place salad on top of toast.
Poach the duck eggs for 3 minutes.
Season and add to the salad.

PRIVATE ACCESS

FISHERMEN
ONLY

MUSSELS

"This soup brings together all the fantastic ingredients from the Marshalls' family farm on the Camel Estuary. The oysters can also be breadcrumbed and deep-fried to add a different texture to the dish."

PORTHILLY SOUP
with Mussels, Clams and Oysters

SERVES 4
PREP: 15-20 mins
COOKING: 90 mins

For the Soup

2	medium mackerel fillets
2	onions
2	carrots
1	red chilli
1	red pepper
4	garlic cloves
1 tbsp	tomato puree
10	ripe tomatoes
1	bay leaf
1	sprig of rosemary
1	orange zest and juice
1L	crab stock

For the Shellfish

150g	clams
150g	mussels
4	oysters *shucked*
100g	samphire

For the Soup
Deseed the chilli and pepper.
Roughly chop, along with the mackerel and other vegetables.
Lightly fry, season well and cover with the stock (retaining 30ml of stock for Shellfish).
Add the herbs, orange juice and zest, then bring to the boil and simmer for 90 minutes.
Blend in a food processor.
Pass through a large sieve.

For the Shellfish
Place the mussels and clams in a hot pan.
Add 30ml of crab stock and cover until they open.
Add the samphire and oysters and gently simmer for 2 minutes.

To serve, spoon the shellfish into four bowls and pour over the soup.

"This humble fish is really tasty and it is sad that restaurants do not celebrate the grey mullet, choosing instead to use the made-up name 'silver mullet' to make menus look more appealing. Watch out for the wonderful bright and fragrant yellow oil which slowly releases from under the skin when grilling."

GRILLED GREY MULLET
with Cornish Crab and Sweetcorn

SERVES 4
PREP: 30 mins plus 30 mins infusing
COOKING: 10 mins

4	grey mullet fillets
4	corn on the cob
200ml	double cream
200ml	milk
8 tbsp	picked white crab meat
2 tbsp	chopped chives
50g	butter
	salt

Remove sweetcorn kernals from the husk, place in a pan and cover with milk and cream.
Bring to the boil and remove from heat.
Allow to infuse for 30 minutes.
Pass through a sieve, retaining both the corn kernals and infused cream.
In a separate pan, melt the butter and gently fry half the sweetcorn nibs until soft.
Cover the kernals with the infused sweetcorn cream.
Bring to the boil.
Blend in a food processor and pass through a sieve using the back of a spoon.
Stir in the chopped chives and add a pinch of salt.
Mix the other half of the sweetcorn kernals with the picked white crab.
Grill the grey mullet fillets.

To serve, place two tablespoons of the crab and sweetcorn mixture on the plate and pour over the sweetcorn sauce.

Season the grey mullet fillets and place on top.

"This beautiful fish is at its best cooked whole on a barbecue or a chargrill because the strong, meaty flavour takes on the smokiness so well."

CHARGRILLED RED GURNARD
with Saffron Mayonnaise and Tomatoes

SERVES 4
PREP: 20-30 mins
COOKING: 10-15 mins

4 medium-sized red gurnard
fins trimmed and gutted

For the Tomatoes
10 plum tomatoes
1 shallot
1 garlic clove
chopped dill

For the Saffron Mayonnaise
3 egg yolks
pinch of saffron
1 tbsp white wine vinegar
10g English mustard
250ml rapeseed oil

For the Tomatoes
Chop the tomatoes, shallots and garlic.
Mix together in a pan and cook to a thick purée.
Season to taste and add a sprinkle of chopped dill.

For the Saffron Mayonnaise
Whisk the egg yolks, saffron, vinegar and mustard together until well combined.
Whisk continually, adding the rapeseed oil a little at a time, until the mayonnaise is a smooth glossy consistency.

Chargrill the fish and serve with a good spoonful of the purée and saffron mayonnaise.

PZ 643
PZ243
PZ243
FH514

PAUL AINSWORTH

"I moved to Cornwall from London seven years ago, fresh-faced and very naïve. I didn't really know what a food season was - in Cornwall when it's in season you use it; when it's gone, it's gone. For that I owe Cornwall so much. It's taught me the true meaning of great ingredients and when they are at their best."

"Cornish oysters and Cornish salami are brought together with a fresh lime and fennel salad. This recipe really shows what we have on our doorstep down here in Cornwall."

CRISPY OYSTERS & CORNISH SALAMI
with Fennel and Lime Salad

MAKES 12
PREP: 30 mins
COOKING: 5 mins

For the Salad

1	large bulb of fennel
2	Granny Smith apples
2	limes
2 tbsp	caster sugar
	chervil

For the Oysters

12	oysters *as fresh as possible*
3	egg whites *gently mixed together*
200g	breadcrumbs *panko are best*
12	finely-cut slices of salami
	sea salt
	olive oil

For the Salad
Zest the two limes using a very fine grater. Juice both the limes and add in the zest and sugar.
Heat in a saucepan with lid removed, until reduced by three-quarters.
Allow the reduced fluid to cool whilst preparing the apple and fennel.
Trim the tops and root from the fennel.
Split the fennel in half, exposing the heart.
Use fingers to prise apart the individual layers, then peel off the outer film.
Slice the layers of fennel lengthways, as thinly as possible, approximately matchstick size.
Peel and cut the apple into thin slices, then cut into matchstick-sized batons to match the size of the fennel matchsticks.
Mix the fennel and apple matchsticks with the lime reduction, adding chervil to taste. Set aside.

For the Oysters
Preheat oil to 180°C-200°C, preferably in a deep-fat fryer.
Open the oysters and wash them, then pat dry gently, but thoroughly, on kitchen paper.
Clean shells thoroughly, removing all grit and stringy bits.
When the oysters are dry, dip in the egg white, shake off any excess, then place in the breadcrumbs.
Move gently in the breadcrumbs until each oyster is evenly coated, gently shaking off any excess.
Check temperature of oil before dropping oysters into the basket and fry until the breadcrumbs are golden and the oysters not quite cooked through. Drain onto kitchen paper to remove excess oil.
Season with sea salt.

To finish, place a portion of the apple, lime and fennel salad in the cleaned oyster shell. Put a golden-coated oyster on top. The oyster should be 'plump' side up. Place one very fine slice of salami on top of each oyster. Finish with a drizzle of olive oil.

AIR DRIED CHARCUTERIE

HAND DIVED SCALLOPS

"Whenever I am having scallops at home, this is the simplest and most lovely way of doing them: grilled simply with butter, lemon and seasoning. In this recipe, the brown shrimps and parsley give them a little extra 'something' along with the crunchy croutons."

CORNISH SCALLOPS
with Brown Shrimp Butter

SERVES 4
PREP: 10-15 mins
COOKING: 5 mins

4	large scallops
250g	butter
250g	brown shrimps
100g	freshly-chopped chervil *keep 25g back for finishing*
pinch of	ground mace
1	lemon - juice only
	sea salt
	white pepper, milled
2	slices of fresh brioche
	a knob of butter for frying

Remove the scallops from their shells, saving the dome part of the shell.
If desired, remove orange coral.
Wash the scallops lightly in a bowl of cold water and drain them on kitchen paper. Place in the fridge until serving.

For the Butter
Soften the butter to a paste but do not melt.
Add the brown shrimps and chervil and then the lemon, mace and seasoning to taste.
Mix well and place the butter mixture on a sheet of cling film.
Roll into a cylinder roughly the same circumference as the scallops.
Chill the butter in the fridge.

Cut the brioche slices into bite-size cubes.
Lightly fry them in a frying pan with a knob of butter and seasoning.
When they are golden in colour, drain them and leave to cool on a tray lined with kitchen paper.
Put each scallop into a shell, lightly season and drizzle with olive oil.
Place under the grill for about 2 minutes – or more, depending on size.
Unwrap the butter and slice into 1cm pieces.
Place a slice of butter on top of each scallop.
Continue to cook the scallops until the butter has turned nut brown.
The scallops should be a little firm to the touch, but not hard.

To serve, add more chopped chervil and the crunchy croutons.

DEXTER BEEF

"When I am asked what my last meal might be, this Dexter steak and chips with Cornish blue cheese butter and St Enodoc asparagus is a big contender. Now that's what I'm talking about!"

DEXTER RUMP OF BEEF
with Cornish Blue Cheese Butter

SERVES 4
PREP: 20-30 mins
COOKING: 45 mins, including resting

4	250g Dexter rump steaks
6	large Maris Piper potatoes *peeled and cut into chunky chips about 2cm x 8cm*
16	spears of St Enodoc asparagus *with woody ends removed*
250g	unsalted butter
100g	Cornish blue cheese *at room temperature*
	sea salt
	milled white pepper
	splash of sherry vinegar
50g	flat leaf parsley *chopped*
	vegetable oil for the deep fat fryer

Trim the steaks of any excess fat and gristle. Leave them to come up to room temperature.

Heat the oil in a deep-fat fryer to 120°C.
Place the cut chips in the basket and blanch until they are completely soft. Remove them from the basket and drain on kitchen paper.
Turn the fryer up to 180°C-200°C.

Soften the butter and mix it with the soft blue cheese. Season to taste and add the sherry vinegar and parsley. Place the butter on a sheet of cling film. Roll into a cylinder the size of a £2 coin and set the butter in the fridge.

Take a shallow, wide-bottom saucepan; add a little water and a knob of butter. Season with salt and pepper and add the asparagus to the pan. Shake the pan occasionally to roll the asparagus - the water and the butter will thicken and coat it. This process will take about 3 minutes. Leave the asparagus in the pan to keep warm.

Heat a large frying pan. It needs to get really hot and should accommodate the size of the steaks. Add a little vegetable oil to the pan when it starts to smoke. Season the steaks with salt and pepper and add carefully to the pan. Do not shake the pan or move the steaks until the first side is caramelised. Turn the steaks over and do the same again. Add a little butter to the pan and allow it to turn nut brown. Baste the steak and cook according to preference - medium-rare should take about 4-5 minutes from the steak going into the pan.

Lift the steaks out and rest for at least 10 minutes on a rack with a plate underneath to catch any juices. After 5 minutes of resting, turn the steak over and rest for another 5 minutes.

Return the chips to the fryer and cook until golden and crisp. Drain, season and divide between the plates. Serve the asparagus next to the chips.

Slice a piece of the chilled butter on each steak. Warm the steaks through in either the oven or grill to lightly soften the butter. Serve immediately.

CLOTTED CREAM

"My Cornish take on sticky toffee pudding is helped along with generous amounts of Cornish fudge and a lovely scoop of cold clotted cream against the warm pudding."

STICKY CORNISH FUDGE PUDDING
with Clotted Cream

SERVES 4
PREP: 20-30 mins
COOKING: 40 mins

For the Pudding

175g	stoned dates
300ml	water
1 tsp	bicarbonate of soda
50g	unsalted butter
175g	soft dark brown sugar
2	eggs
175g	self-raising flour
250g	good-quality Cornish fudge *diced into small pieces*

For the Sauce

100g	soft light brown sugar
100g	unsalted butter
150ml	double cream

For the Pudding
Preheat oven to 180°C.
In a large mixing bowl, beat together the butter and sugar until thoroughly combined and creamy.
Add the eggs slowly, beating well after each addition.
Put the water and dates in a saucepan and bring to the boil.
Add the bicarbonate of soda.
Blend with a stick blender or in a food processor.
Combine the two mixtures thoroughly.
Gently fold in the flour, again making sure everything is mixed well.
Add in half of the diced fudge.
Butter a deep baking tray, then line with greaseproof paper.
Pour the mix into the tray and bake for 35-40 minutes: it should be just firm to the touch.

For the Sauce
Put all ingredients into a pan and heat gently until the sugar has completely dissolved.
Simmer until it turns a beautiful golden colour.

To serve, pour a little of the sauce over each piece of pudding and finish with a good scattering of the remaining tiny fudge pieces.

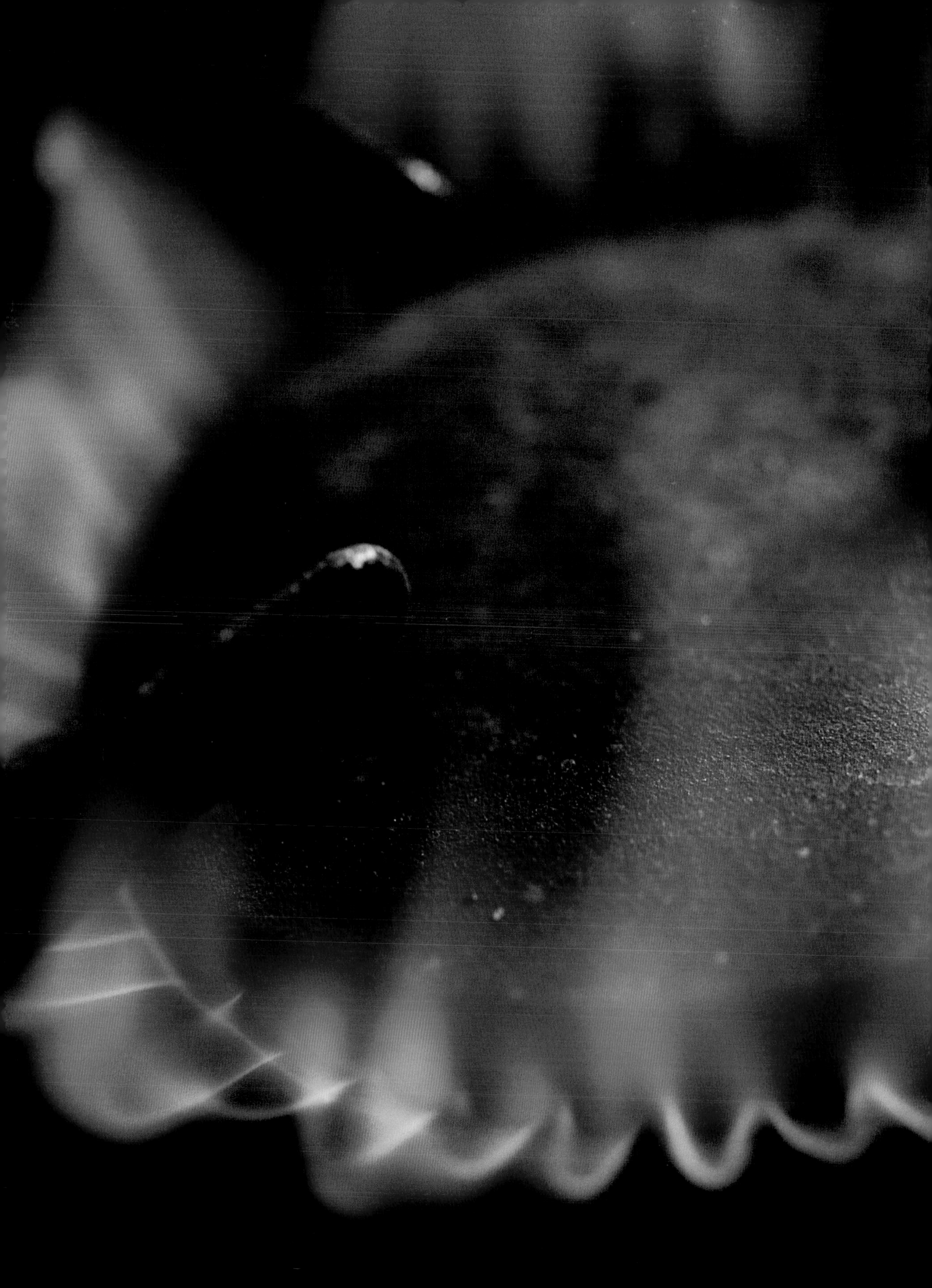

PW132

JACK STEIN

"Being born and brought up in Cornwall, some of my earliest memories are of the seashore, picking mussels and winkles and watching Dad cook them. Although I have been away to study and to work in other establishments, I am very fortunate in being able to return and work where I grew up. I cannot live away from the ocean for too long and the harvest which it bestows upon us makes my job a pleasure!"

CURRIED POLLOCK
with Sweetcorn

MAKES 8 CANAPES
PREP: 20 mins
COOKING: 15 mins

200g pollock fillet
300g tinned sweetcorn *drained*
75ml chicken stock or water
30g butter
salt
pinch of garam masala
knob of butter

For the Sweetcorn
Drain the sweetcorn and place with stock, butter and salt into a pan.
Boil for 3 minutes.
Remove from the heat and allow to cool for a few minutes.
Blend in a food processor.
Pass the mixture through a sieve, using the back of a spoon, to make a fine purée.
Put the purée into a pan and stir in the garam masala.
Check seasoning and keep warm.

For the Pollock
Remove the skin from the pollock and cut into bite-size pieces.
Fry in a hot, non-stick pan on one side until almost cooked through.
Add a knob of butter and season well with salt and a pinch of the garam masala.
Turn the pollock and serve brown side up.

To serve, place a small amount of the purée onto a canapé spoon (or a large crouton) and place the fish on top.

"This is a take on a traditional Cornish dish of tea pickled herring. Variants of this dish can be found all over the county, from Newlyn to Bude, differing in spice mixes or aromats. Soda bread is a traditional Celtic fringe staple that is an easy first homemade bread to try."

TEA PICKLED MACKEREL *with Soda Bread*

SERVES 4
PREP: 15 mins plus 10 mins salting
COOKING: 1½ hours

For the Mackerel

8	mackerel fillets
200ml	cider vinegar
50ml	Assam tea
50g	shallots *peeled*
½ tsp	thyme
½ tsp	fennel seeds
1	lime *zested*
30g	demerara sugar
5 slices	medium red chilli
1	bay leaf
	salt
	vegetable oil
	knob of butter for frying

For the Bread

250g	plain flour
5g	baking soda
5g	salt
15g	sugar
235g	yogurt

For the Mackerel

Combine all the ingredients, except the mackerel, in a pan and bring to the boil.
Remove from the heat and leave to infuse for at least an hour – creating a pickle.
Salt the mackerel fillets on the flesh side and leave for 10 minutes.
Pour the pickle into a tray.
Wash the salt off the mackerel.
Place flesh-side down in the pickle.
Leave for 20 minutes.
Pat the skin dry and fry in vegetable oil skin side down, adding a little butter as the flesh starts to become opaque.
Warm some of the pickled shallots and some of the pickling liquor and spoon over the fillets.

For the Bread

Mix the dry ingredients together and add the yogurt to form a dough.
Remove from the bowl and place on a lightly-floured work surface.
Knead the dough for 5 minutes.
Lightly oil a large skillet or frying pan and place on a medium heat.
Divide the dough into two pieces.
Use a rolling pin to roll each piece until it is about 2cm thick.
Use a sharp knife and score the dough into quarters, cut 1-1½cm deep.
Place the dough in the pan, score side down, and cook for 8 minutes.
Turn over and cook for a further 8 minutes.
The bread is cooked when the sides spring back after being pressed.

To finish, warm the soda bread and serve with the mackerel.

"During the Age of Sail, Padstow was a very important port on the way to the Americas, and a staple on board such voyages would have been salted pork and beef. This was purely a preservative measure, but modern-day cooks have discovered benefits in the kitchen of salting meat. Using a weak brine, muscle fibres begin to swell and absorb water, resulting in a meat that is both more tender and more tasty."

BRINED PORK COLLAR
with Mushy Peas and Mint

SERVES 4
PREP: 45 mins
CHILL: Overnight
COOKING: 1½ hours

For the Pork Brine

1.5kg	pork collar on the bone
3.5L	water
420g	salt
210g	sugar
35g	yellow mustard seeds
50g	crushed garlic
10g	fennel seeds

For the Mushy Peas

500g	marrowfat peas
18g	bicarbonate of soda
2.5L	water
100g	butter
12g	Marmite
15ml	Worcestershire sauce
5g	salt

For the Mint Sauce

5g	demerara sugar
15g	mint leaves
20ml	cider vinegar
	salt to season

For the Pork Brine
Put all the brining ingredients (except the pork) in a large saucepan.
Bring to the boil. Remove from the heat and whisk vigorously until all the salt and sugar has dissolved.
Chill the brine and then fully submerge the pork collar.
Leave overnight.

For the Mushy Peas
Place the marrowfat peas into a bowl.
Add 10g of bicarbonate of soda and 1.5L of water.
Mix well and leave at room temperature for 10 hours.
Rinse well in cold water.
Mix the peas with 1L of water and 8g of bicarbonate of soda.
Place on a high heat and bring to the boil.
Simmer for about 15 minutes until tender, skimming any excess skins from the top. Mash slightly with a fork.
Add butter, Marmite, Worcestershire sauce and salt.

To cook the Pork
Preheat oven to 220°C.
Remove the pork from the brine and rinse in fresh water.
Place the pork in a large roasting tin and roast for the first 20 minutes.
Lower the temperature to 180°C for a further 1 hour or until the internal temperature is at 66°C.
Remove from the oven and rest for 30 minutes.

For the Mint Sauce
Roughly chop the mint.
Place it in a mortar and pestle along with the salt, sugar and vinegar.
Combine all the ingredients.

PICK
YOUR
OWN

"Once upon a time, the word 'fairing' referred to any edible treat or gift sold at feast and fair days both in Cornwall and elsewhere in England. Over time, the name has become associated with gingerbread or ginger biscuits. Cornish fairings are sweet and spicy ginger biscuits and are as important to us as clotted cream and pasties."

STRAWBERRY & ELDERFLOWER FOOL *with Cornish Fairings*

SERVES 6
PREP: 25 mins
COOKING: 15 mins plus cooling

For the Fairings

225g	plain flour
½ tsp	salt
1 tsp	baking powder
1 tsp	bicarbonate of soda
10g	mixed spice
15g	ginger
5g	cinnamon
125g	butter
125g	sugar
120g	golden syrup

For the Fool

300ml	double cream
75g	clotted cream
200ml	elderflower pressé
400g	strawberries
55g	caster sugar
15ml	lemon juice
pinch of	cracked pepper
5	mint leaves *chopped*

For the Fairings
Preheat the oven to 170°C.
Sieve all the dry ingredients into a bowl - except the sugar.
Rub in the butter until it looks like breadcrumbs.
Add the sugar and mix.
Warm the golden syrup and pour into the dry mix.
Combine it into a smooth dough.
Roll the dough out to about ¾cm thick.
Use a small cookie cutter to cut out the fairings.
Place onto a floured baking tray and bake in the oven until golden brown - about 15 minutes.

For the Fool
Mash half the strawberries with a fork along with the sugar and lemon juice to create a marinade.
Slice the rest of the strawberries and add to the strawberry marinade.
Add the cracked pepper and chopped mint.
Leave to marinate for 15 minutes.
Put the double cream, clotted cream and elderflower pressé into a bowl.
Whip into stiff peaks.

To Serve
Place a layer of marinated strawberries in the bottom of a glass and then a layer of cream.
Repeat until you reach the top of the glass.
Crumble some Cornish fairings over the top for texture.

SAM MOODY

"As a chef, living in Bath is perfect - near rich seas full of beautiful fish; livestock grazing on lush pasture; friendly cows; the odd crazy goat; and fantastic pubs filled with real ale drinkers. Here, everyone wants to eat great food and, with so many local people making it their life's work to create quality produce, it's a very exciting place to be."

"Oysters were once a plentiful staple of the Victorian lower classes and used to bulk out dishes such as pies, soups and stews. This recipe uses these now highly prized shellfish to create a rich, tasty and fun British classic with a twist."

BEEF AND OYSTER PIES *with Ale*

SERVES 4
PREP: 45 mins
COOKING: 2-3 hrs

500g	puff pastry
12	oysters
1	large beef cheek *trimmed*
1	carrot *medium rough diced*
2	sticks of celery *medium rough diced*
1	small onion *medium rough diced*
1	leek *medium rough diced*
5	ripe tomatoes *chopped*
2	cloves of garlic *crushed*
3	sprigs of thyme
1	bay leaf
1	large glass of ale
	chicken stock to cover

Preheat the oven to 140°C.
Very lightly season the beef cheek with salt and pepper.
Use an ovenproof casserole dish on the hob and caramelise all the sides of the beef cheek.
Set aside the beef cheek and reduce the heat on the casserole dish.
Add the vegetables to the pot and sweat over a gentle heat for 10-15 minutes.
Add the tomatoes and cook for another 10 minutes.
Add the ale and reduce by half.
Return the caramelised beef cheek to the casserole dish and top with chicken stock.
Bring to a light simmer and cover with foil.
Transfer to the oven and braise for 2-3 hours, or until the beef cheek is soft but not falling apart.
Allow the cheek to cool slowly in the liquid.
Once cold, remove the cheek and pull apart into small pieces.
Pass the liquid through a colander and reduce in a saucepan to the consistency of a light gravy.
Pour half the liquid back onto the small pieces of beef cheek.
Allow to cool and then refrigerate.
Preheat the oven to 170°C.
Open the oysters - clean both oysters and their shells well.
Place each oyster back into its shell and top with the braised beef mix.
Roll out the puff pastry and cover each shell.
Lightly egg wash and then cook for 15-18 minutes, until golden.

OXFORD SANDY AND BLACK PIG

"Bath chaps are a traditional Somerset dish and one of my most favourite things to eat. They are a brilliant way to use up a part of the animal that might not otherwise be used. To cut through the fat, these are best served with a pickle or a good-quality wholegrain mustard."

BATH CHAPS
Cured Pigs' Cheeks

SERVES 8
PREP: 20 mins
COOKING: 3½ hrs
CHILLING: Overnight

4	pigs' cheeks *off the bone with the skin removed*
2L	cider
1	onion *medium rough diced*
3	apples *medium rough diced*
1	stick of celery *medium rough diced*
1	carrot *medium rough diced*
4	cloves of garlic
1	sprig of thyme
1 tsp	ground caraway
50ml	white wine vinegar
	slug of olive oil
1 cup	plain flour
1	egg *beaten*
1 cup	breadcrumbs
	oil for deep-frying

Season the pigs' cheeks all over with salt and black pepper.
Preheat a flat, heavy-based casserole dish.
Add the oil and then the cheeks - colour evenly to a light golden brown.
Remove the cheeks from the casserole dish and set to one side.
Lower the heat.
Add the caraway and the roughly diced onion, apples, celery, carrot, garlic and thyme.
Cook the vegetables for about15 minutes until soft.
Preheat the oven to 140°C.
Add the vinegar and reduce by half.
Add the cider and return the cheeks to the casserole dish.
Bring to a light simmer and skim off any scum.
Cover with foil and cook in the oven for 2-3 hours.
Use a small knife to check the cooking – it should feel like pushing the tip of a knife into a pack of butter: firm but no resistance.
Allow to cool for an hour in the stock and then carefully remove.
Roll each cheek tightly in cling film and tie the ends off with twine.
Refrigerate overnight - they will keep for one week and freeze very well at this stage.
After 12 hours (or more), remove the cling film.
Cut each cheek into three.
Place each piece into flour, then egg and finally breadcrumbs.
Deep-fry at 180°C until golden brown.

"A good crab tart is simply perfection: warming in winter and fresh in the summer. It's my idea of food heaven!"

GLAZED TARTLETS *of Brixham Crab*

SERVES 6
PREP: 10-15 mins
COOKING: 20 mins

6 blind baked tartlet cases

For the Crab Filling
300g picked white crab meat
1 tbsp capers
tarragon
finely chopped
squeeze of lemon

For the Hollandaise Sauce
250g butter
melted
4 egg yolks
50ml white wine vinegar
5 black peppercorns
tarragon stalk

For the Crab Filling
Place all the crab ingredients in a bowl and mix together.

For the Hollandaise Sauce
Melt the butter very gently - do not brown.
In a separate pan add the vinegar, peppercorns and tarragon stalk.
Simmer until reduced by half.
Allow the vinegar mix to cool, remove the peppercorns and tarragon stalk and add to the egg yolks.
Whisk the egg yolks and vinegar over a pan of simmering (not boiling) water until the mixture has thickened but not scrambled.
Remove from the heat.
Add the melted butter slowly - whisking constantly and taking care not to add the butter too quickly.
Check the seasoning and fold half of the hollandaise into the crab.

To finish, fill the tartlets with the crab mix. Spoon over the rest of the hollandaise and glaze under a hot grill.

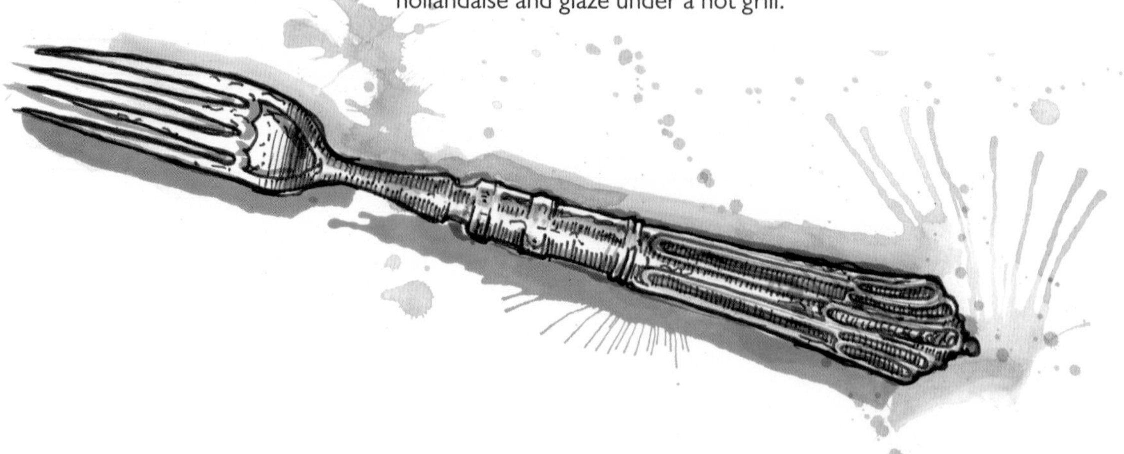

CHEDDAR
CHEESE
Cave aged

"This is the best afternoon snack ever. Try varying it by using different cheeses - we make truck-loads of these in the South West!"

CHEDDAR CHEESE SCONES
with Rhubarb Chutney

SERVES 4
PREP: 30 mins plus 20 mins resting
COOKING: 1½ hrs plus cooling time

For the Scones

375g	plain flour
100g	unsalted butter *softened*
20g	baking powder
1	egg
110ml	milk
200g	grated Cheddar cheese

For the Chutney

500g	rhubarb *chopped into 2cm squares*
1	small onion *finely chopped*
100ml	sherry vinegar
200g	demerara sugar
	olive oil

For the Scones

Rub the baking powder, flour and butter together until it resembles bread-crumbs.
Add the egg, followed by the milk.
Add the cheese and mix well.
Roll out to 3cms thick.
Cut out the scones with a 60mm cutter.
Re-roll the trimmings and repeat.
Place the scones onto a baking tray and lightly cover in cling film.
Rest for 20 minutes.
Preheat the oven to 170°C.
Egg wash the scones and bake for 12-15 minutes.

For the Chutney

Gently sweat the onion in a little olive oil until light in colour.
Add the rhubarb and sugar.
Cook over a gentle heat for 1 hour.
Add the vinegar and sugar.
Cook down to a thick consistency.
Place in a jar and cool.

To serve, warm the Cheddar cheese scones, and top with the chutney and some more Cheddar.

RUSSELL BROWN

"I've lived in the West Country nearly all of my life and was lucky to grow up in a household where food was genuinely important. One of my strong childhood memories is of the 6-8lb enamel bowls of clotted cream sold in my parents' farm shop, the thick golden crust giving way to the sweet, rich cream – delicious! I came late to cooking as a career, but have been hugely inspired by some of the amazing produce available in the region."

"This soup is good on its own but the other ingredients take it to another level, adding textures and different temperatures. The curd cheese is both creamy and tangy and a good contrast to the sweetness of the peas."

PEA AND WHITE WINE SOUP
with Goats' Curd

SERVES 4
PREP: 5-10 mins
COOKING: 30 mins

For the Soup

500g	frozen petits pois
1	large shallot *sliced*
1	stick of celery *sliced*
150ml	white wine
300ml	vegetable stock
	single cream to taste
10g	salt
10g	sugar

To Serve

150g	fresh goats' curd
40g	fresh peas (raw if sweet)
	punnet of pea shoots
	extra virgin olive oil

In a medium, heavy-based pan, sweat the shallot and celery until soft.
Add the wine and reduce until syrupy.
Add the stock and reduce the liquid by a third.
Remove the pan from the heat and allow the soup base to cool.
Add the salt and sugar to boiling water and cook the peas in 3 batches.
Transfer the peas to iced water.
Drain the peas and combine with the soup base.
Blend in a food processor until smooth - do this in fairly small batches and with a sharp blade in order to keep as much colour as possible.
Pass the soup through a fine sieve into a clean pan and heat without boiling.
Adjust the seasoning and consistency as desired.
Add a little cream if the soup is too sharp.
Pour the soup into 4 bowls.

Before serving, add the goats' curd, peas and pea shoots. Finish with a good drizzle of extra virgin olive oil.

"There is an abundance of wild venison across the South West and all the breeds will work for this dish but my particular favourite is Sika for its more open texture and robust flavour."

PEPPERED VENISON LOIN
with Celeriac

SERVES 4 as a starter
PREP: 30 mins plus 1 hour salting for celeriac
CHILL: Overnight
COOKING: 15 mins

For the Venison
350g trimmed venison loin
2 tbsp coarsely ground black pepper
1 tsp sea salt
3 tbsp olive oil
20g unsalted butter

For the Celeriac
1 small celeriac
2 tbsp mayonnaise
3 tbsp crème fraîche
1 tsp Dijon mustard
1 tsp sea salt

To Serve
50g wild rocket

For the Venison
Wrap the venison loin tightly in cling film and then in foil.
Twist the ends tightly to create a compact cylinder.
Refrigerate overnight.
Preheat the oven to 200°C.
Mix the coarsely ground black pepper with the sea salt.
Sprinkle the pepper mix over a chopping board.
Unwrap the venison loin and then roll it across the pepper mix.
In a large frying pan or a roasting tray, heat the olive oil on a medium to high heat.
Sear the venison all over, caramelising well.
Add the butter and baste.
Place the venison in the oven for 2 minutes - turning the loin halfway through.
Remove and place on a cooling rack.
Rest for 10 minutes and chill for at least an hour.

For the Celeriac
Peel the celeriac and cut into thin slices, then cut again into matchstick-size pieces.
Sprinkle sea salt over the celeriac and stir together - leave for 1 hour.
Wash celeriac well and squeeze in a clean cloth to dry thoroughly.
Dress with the mayonnaise, mustard and crème fraîche and season to taste.

To Serve
Slice the chilled venison thinly and sprinkle with a little sea salt.
Dress the rocket leaves with a little olive oil and serve with the celeriac.

"Of all the flat fish, brill is at the top of my list: good texture, delicate sweet flavour and often keenly priced. Buy a 2-3kg fish if you can for nice thick fillets and a good yield."

FILLET OF BRILL
with a Chive Butter Sauce

SERVES 4
PREP: 15 mins
COOKING: 30 mins

4	120g brill fillets *skinned*
500g	new potatoes *washed / scraped*
20	spears of English asparagus *peeled and washed*
25ml	dry vermouth
50ml	white wine
200ml	vegetable stock
25g	unsalted butter for potatoes
20g	unsalted butter for brill *enough to thicken for sauce and a knob for asparagus*
1 tsp	chives *finely chopped*
2 tbsp	olive oil
	sea salt and black pepper
	plain flour for dusting

Cook the potatoes in boiling salted water until tender.
Drain and add the unsalted butter.
Crush the potatoes with a fork - do not work into a mash.
Adjust the seasoning and add more butter if a little dry. Keep warm.

In a small pan, reduce the vermouth and white wine to syrup.
Add the stock and reduce to approximately 50ml.
Whisk in enough cold, unsalted butter to thicken slightly.

Cook the asparagus in boiling salted water until just tender.
Drain and add a knob of butter.

In a large (or two medium) heavy non-stick pan heat the olive oil.
Season the flesh side of the brill fillets and dust lightly with flour.
Place in the pan flour side down.
Cook until golden brown on the flesh side and season the skin side.
Add approximately 20g unsalted butter to the pan.
Baste the fish with the foaming butter.
Turn the brill over and remove from the pan.

Warm the sauce and add the chives. Serve with the crushed new potatoes and asparagus spears.

"One of my strong childhood memories is of the 6-8lb enamel bowls of clotted cream sold in my parents' farm shop, the thick golden crust giving way to the sweet, rich cream - delicious! Done up into its little ¼lb pots, there was strangely always a little left over that needed eating up!"

CLOTTED CREAM SHORTBREAD
Petits Fours

SERVES 4
PREP: 15 mins plus one hour chilling
COOKING: 8 mins

250g	pastry flour
1 tsp	fine ground sea salt
½ tsp	baking powder
110g	caster sugar
125g	clotted cream
90g	soft unsalted butter
½	vanilla pod
2	large free - range egg yolks

Beat the butter with the sugar until pale.
Beat in the cream and the seeds from the vanilla pod.
Gradually add the egg yolks.
In a separate bowl, sift together the flour, salt and baking powder.
Tip the flour onto a clean work surface.
Make a well in the centre - add the cream mix.
Using fingertips, stir together gently and knead briefly into a dough.
Divide into two and roll each half into a sausage approximate 2cm in diameter.
Wrap tightly in cling film and chill for at least an hour.
Preheat the oven to 165°C.
Remove the cling film and slice the dough into rounds approximately 5mm thick.
Place on a baking sheet lined with silicone or greaseproof paper, leaving at least 1cm between biscuits.
Bake for approximately 8 minutes or until pale golden brown.
Remove from the oven and sprinkle with light brown sugar.

Allow to cool before serving.

"This vanilla cream is so versatile. The flavour of the cream or fruit can be changed according to the season - a ginger cream with poached pear or a coffee cream with caramelised orange are two lovely variations."

SET VANILLA CREAM
with Cider Poached Apple

SERVES 8
PREP: 30 mins
COOKING: 1 hour
CHILL: 1 hour

For the Pannacotta

350g	double cream
175g	semi - skimmed milk
1	vanilla pod
55g	caster sugar
2	leaves of gelatine *soaked in cold water*

For the Apple

2	Granny Smith apples *peeled and cut into balls with a melon baller*
30g	caster sugar
250ml	dry cider
8	peppercorns
1	cinnamon stick

For the Pannacotta
Put the cream, sugar and milk in a medium saucepan.
Split the vanilla pod and scrape out the seeds.
Add to the cream.
Scald the cream mix and leave to infuse for 45 minutes.
Squeeze out the gelatine and add to the infused cream.
Re-warm the cream mix to dissolve if necessary.
Pour the pannacotta mix through a fine sieve into a jug – pushing down well on the vanilla.
Place the jug into an ice bath to cool - stirring frequently.
When the mix begins to thicken, pour into moulds and chill to set.

For the Apple
Heat the sugar in a small heavy pan to form a dark caramel.
In a separate pan, heat the cider and spices.
Carefully pour the hot cider over the caramel and stir until dissolved.
Reduce to approximately 150ml and strain into a clean pan.
Add the apple balls and heat until just simmering.
Remove from the heat and allow to cool.
Drain and reduce the caramel to form a light syrup.

To serve, turn the set vanilla on to a plate and add the apple and syrup.

"The produce in Devon and Cornwall continues to be first class – the region is full of passionate producers who really care about their products. We feel very lucky to have made such good friends with these producers, and also other chefs, who continue to fly the flag for the West Country."

T
TANNERS

"This is a fantastic way to eat a humble piece of pork and the treacle adds a comforting element. You will need to prepare this dish 24 hours in advance before serving."

TREACLE BRUSHED PORK BELLY
with a Devon Cider Sauce

SERVES 4
PREP: 30-40 mins
CHILL: Overnight
COOKING: 3¼ hrs

1.2kg	un-scored boneless pork belly
1L	fresh chicken stock
	splash of cider vinegar
2	garlic cloves *smashed*
2	celery sticks *chopped*
1	onion *chopped*
1	carrot *chopped*
1	bay leaf
	sprig of thyme
	black treacle *to brush onto pork*
	small knob of unsalted butter

Preheat the oven to 180°C.
Place all the ingredients except the pork and treacle into a large saucepan and bring to the boil.
Gently season the pork with salt and pepper and place into a deep casserole dish.
Pour the remaining ingredients over the pork until completely submerged.
Top up with a little water if necessary.
Cover with a tight - fitting lid or tin foil and place in the oven for about 3 hours.
When the pork is cooked, leave it to cool slightly in the stock.
Line a flat tray with cling film.
Carefully remove the pork from the liquor and remove any bits of vegetables or herbs.
Place the pork onto the cling film and cover with another piece of cling film.
Place a flat tray on top. Weigh the pork down with another dish or some cans. Leave to cool in the fridge overnight.
Strain the remaining cooking liquor into a jug and refrigerate.
The following day, unwrap the pork and place onto a board.
Trim the remaining edges and cut the pork into serving - size portions.
Preheat the oven to 180°C.
Heat a non-stick pan on the stove.
Place the pork in skin side down – carefully, as it has a tendency to spit.
Sizzle the pork (like bacon) for about 5 minutes until golden brown.
Add a little of the cooking liquor.
Brush the pork liberally with the treacle.
Place the pork in the oven and heat through for 5 minutes.
Remove from the oven and place onto a warmed dish.
Add a little more of the cooking liquor to the pan and bring to the boil.
Remove from the heat and whisk in a small knob of cold butter.
Serve immediately.

SPUDS
5-50

"This dish never dates. The duck legs will keep in their own fat refrigerated for up to 1 month, or 3 months in the freezer, so make sure you always cook a few extra. To reheat the legs, remove from the fat and place in an ovenproof dish, skin side down. Roast for 30 minutes at 200°C, turning halfway through, until crisp and brown. This dish works really well with braised lentils or pearl barley and is a favourite comfort food of ours."

CONFIT DUCK
with a Herb Gratin Crumb

SERVES 4
PREP: 30 mins
CHILL: Overnight
COOKING: 3-4 hours

4	duck legs
1	handful of coarse sea salt
2	bay leaves *roughly torn*
5	garlic cloves *smashed*
1	handful of thyme sprigs
100ml	white wine
150g	white breadcrumbs
1	handful of chopped herbs parsley, chervil and chives

Scatter half the salt, two smashed cloves of garlic and half the herbs over the base of a shallow dish.
Lay the duck legs, skin side up, on top and scatter over the remaining salt, two more smashed cloves of garlic and herbs.
Cover the duck and refrigerate overnight - this can be done up to 2 days in advance.
Preheat the oven to 165°C.
Pour the wine into an ovenproof saucepan – large enough to fit in all the duck legs.
Brush the salt off the duck legs and place them skin side down into the wine.
Cover with a lid and place over a medium heat.
Once the wine starts to bubble, transfer to the oven and cook for about 3-4 hours.
Check during the cooking process – after an hour or so the legs should be submerged in their own fat.
After 3 hours the meat should feel tender when touched.
Remove from the oven and allow the legs to cool in their own fat.
For the gratin - place the breadcrumbs, one garlic clove and herbs in a food processor and blend.
Spoon a generous amount over each duck leg and brown under a grill.

"This is a simple but elegant way of enjoying a truly underrated fish. Mackerel has a fantastic flavour, and with this recipe we have just enhanced it with the ginger and thyme butter. When we opened our first restaurant it featured on our lunch menu and it continues to be a firm favourite many years on."

GRILLED FILLETS OF MACKEREL
with a Ginger and Thyme Butter

SERVES 4
PREP: 10 mins
COOKING: 6-8 mins

4	fresh mackerel *filleted and boned*
1 tbsp	fresh chopped thyme
75g	chopped stem ginger
100g	unsalted butter
	sea salt
	squeeze of lemon

Place the mackerel fillets on a baking tray.
Season with a little sea salt.
Soften the butter, add the ginger and thyme and mix well.
Spread the butter mix over the mackerel fillets.
Grill each side for 3-4 minutes.
To serve, arrange the mackerel fillets on a plate.
Spoon over any excess juices from the tray.

Finish with a squeeze of fresh lemon.

"Turbot is definitely one of the kings of the sea. Coupled with the delicious crab sauce, this dish will stand out from the crowd at a dinner party."

ROAST FILLET OF TURBOT
with a Crab Cream Sauce

SERVES 4 - 6
PREP: 30-40 mins
COOKING: 1½ hrs

For the Crab Sauce

2kg	crab shells
1	white onion
1	carrot
	peeled and chopped
2	celery stalks
	chopped
50ml	olive oil
2	thyme sprigs
2	bay leaves
4	large overripe tomatoes
	chopped
1 tbsp	tomato paste
pinch of	cayenne pepper
100ml	dry white wine
50ml	brandy
1L	fish stock
500ml	beef stock
	salt and pepper
100ml	cream

For the Turbot

4	large turbot fillet portions
	splash of rapeseed oil
	sea salt
	a squeeze of lemon

For the Crab Sauce

Crush the crab bones with a rolling pin until broken into small pieces.
Fry the onion, carrot and celery in olive oil in a large saucepan.
Cook until slightly coloured.
Add the crab shells (these will be removed later when the soup is passed through a sieve).
Cook for 5 minutes on a medium heat.
Add the herbs and tomatoes - cook for 2 minutes.
Add the tomato paste and cayenne pepper and cook for a further 5 minutes.
Add the wine and brandy and cook for another 5 minutes.
Add the beef and fish stocks and bring to the boil.
Season and simmer for 45 minutes - stirring occasionally.
Strain through a fine sieve and return liquid to a clean saucepan.
Simmer to reduce the liquid by a third.
Add the cream and bring back to the boil.

For the Turbot

Add a little rapeseed oil to a large non-stick frying pan.
Season the fish and carefully place into the pan.
Keep the heat just below high and cook for 3 minutes until golden.
Carefully turn the fish over and cook for a further 1-2 minutes.
Remove the pan from the heat and squeeze a little fresh lemon over the fish. Transfer onto some kitchen paper.

To serve, place the fish on a bed of your favourite green vegetables and add sauce accordingly.

HONEY
3·50 LB

"This is our version of Somerset Apple Cake and is finished with a gentle brushing of Devon blossom honey and brown sugar. A real afternoon treat."

SOMERSET APPLE CAKE
with Devon Blossom Honey

SERVES 4
PREP: 15 mins
COOKING: 1 hour

100g	unsalted butter *at room temperature*
175g	soft brown sugar
2	free-range eggs
225g	plain flour
1 tsp	cinnamon
2 tsp	baking powder
450g	Bramley apples *peeled and chopped*
4 tbsp	milk
	Devon blossom honey

Preheat the oven to 180°C.
Cream the butter and sugar.
Slowly add the beaten eggs.
Sift in the flour, baking powder and cinnamon.
Mix in the milk and fold in the apples.
Bake in a medium cake tin for about 1 hour.
Check to see if the cake is cooked by inserting a knife or skewer into the sponge.
Allow to cool slightly and drizzle or brush with the warmed Devon blossom honey.
Sprinkle a little sugar over the top.

Serve with creamy custard or a dollop of clotted cream.

SS80

MICK SMITH

"It's such an amazing location - I have to pinch myself sometimes when we look out the back door of the kitchen and see the beautiful St Ives Bay. It is great to take a quick stroll down to the waves to fill a large pot with seawater to cook the lobsters in. Being from Australia, I am influenced by Asian cooking – and I have found that the seaweed we forage from the beach works well when cooked with these Asian flavours."

"Sprats are everywhere in the winter. I like to think of them as Cornish anchovies – just get a sharp knife, some salt and some vinegar – result!"

MARINATED CORNISH SPRATS
with Sage, Lime and Saffron

MAKES 12
PREP: 30 mins
COOKING: 10 mins

12	Cornish sprats or anchovies *filleted*
24	sage leaves
2	limes
1 tsp	sea salt
pinch of	saffron

For the Pickle

150ml	white wine vinegar
1 tsp	cracked black pepper
4	cloves
1 tsp	thyme
1 tsp	coriander seeds
	sea salt
1	bay leaf

For the Beer Batter

120g	self-raising flour, plus a little extra for battering
40g	cornflour
	beer to desired consistency
1 tsp	baking powder
pinch of	sea salt

Salt the fillets for 30 minutes.

For the Pickle

Mix the white wine vinegar, pepper, cloves, thyme, coriander seeds and bay leaf.
Pickle the fillets in the vinegar mix for 2 hours.

For the Beer Batter

Mix all dry beer batter ingredients together.
Slowly add beer and gently whisk for 2 minutes.
Rest batter for 5 minutes, then whisk again.

Place each anchovy or sprat between 2 sage leaves.
Flour lightly and dip in the batter.
Deep-fry at 180°C until golden brown – about 2 minutes.
Sprinkle with saffron and sea salt.
Squeeze fresh lime juice over.

"Black mustard grows everywhere in Cornwall - it is a powerful flavour that is similar to wasabi. We adapted this recipe from another that actually used wasabi."

GRILLED OYSTERS
with Black Mustard Mayonnaise

MAKES 24
PREP: 15 mins
COOKING: 6-7 mins

24	shucked Porthilly oysters
1	chorizo sausage *finely diced*

For the Mayonnaise

2	free-range egg yolks
½ tsp	Dijon mustard
25ml	white vinegar
½L	vegetable oil
	juice of half a lemon
	salt and pepper
1 tbsp	wild black mustard cress *chopped*
	black mustard flowers to garnish

For the Mayonnaise

Whisk the yolks and chopped wild black mustard cress until combined.
Continue whisking and slowly add the oil.
When the mixture seems too thick, add some vinegar.
Add lemon juice, salt and pepper to finish.
Refrigerate in a small sealed tub immediately.

To Serve

Preheat oven to 180°C.
Spoon a teaspoon of mayonnaise over each oyster and scatter chorizo over the top.
Grill for 6-7 minutes until the mayonnaise begins to turn brown.
Serve immediately and garnish with black mustard flowers.

"We use cuttlefish when it is in season because not only is it more plentiful and local, but the end result gives a great texture. Use squid instead if you can't get hold of cuttlefish."

CRISPY FRIED CORNISH SQUID
with Black Spices

SERVES 4
PREP: 15 mins
COOKING: 10 mins

For the Squid

60g	cornflour
60g	chickpea flour
2	medium squid
	sea salt
	ground black pepper
	cooking oil

For the Black Spice

makes 1 small jar

2 tbsp	coriander seeds
2 tbsp	nigella seeds
1 tbsp	cardamom
1 tbsp	Szechuan pepper
	pinch of crushed dried chilli

For the Black Spice Mix

Toast the coriander seeds in a pan until they release a perfumed smell.
Set aside.
Toast the cardamom pods in the pan for about 2 minutes.
Allow to cool.
Remove the cardamom seeds from their pods, discarding the pods.
Put the cardamom and coriander seeds into a pestle and mortar with all the other ingredients.
Grind to a fine powder.
Pass through a fine sieve.
Set aside for later.

For the Squid

Mix the cornflour and chickpea flour together.
Heat a deep-fat fryer or large saucepan filled with cooking oil to 190°C.
Rinse the squid under a tap and pat dry with kitchen paper.
Remove the entrails and quill.
Remove and discard the beak from the centre of the tentacles.
Slit each squid up the side to unfold it.
Score the inside with a table knife.
Cut into several triangle-shaped pieces.
Dredge in the flour mix and dust off any excess.
Fry untill crispy and lightly golden brown for about 3-4 minutes.
Carefully drain onto kitchen paper.
Season with salt and pepper, then toss with the black spice mix.

NETTLES

"My friend, Marco, started producing a Cornish cider last year. He provided us with a sample or two, so we tried it with some mussels and a bunch of nettles: the resulting taste was amazing."

STEAMED MUSSELS
with Cornish Cider and Nettles

SERVES 4
PREP: 15 mins
COOKING: 5 mins

800g	mussels
100g	crème fraîche
250ml	fish stock
20	cherry tomatoes
4	cloves of garlic
330ml	Cornish cider
12	basil leaves
1 tbsp	fresh fennel - diced
1	shallot - finely diced
100g	unsalted butter
20	nettle leaves

Heat the butter in a large pan.
Sweat the fennel, shallots and garlic until soft.
Add the mussels, fish stock and cider.
Cover and cook on a high temperature for 3 minutes.
Add the cherry tomatoes and nettles.
Cook for a further 2 minutes or until all the shells are open.
Add the crème fraîche and basil and stir through.
Serve with crusty bread.

TOM KERRIDGE

"Growing up in the West Country is something that I am very proud of – some of my greatest childhood memories are connected to the food of the region. The area is full of real people with a love and passion for everything around them, including the rivers, countryside and coastal areas."

H&T

"This is a firm favourite of everyone at the restaurant. It is a perfect lunch dish as it is everything in one – meat and great pastry."

PORK PIE
with Thyme and Pepper

SERVES 8
PREP: 1½ hours
COOKING: 1½ hours
CHILL: 24 hours for jelly and further 24 hours for setting

Pork Pie Filling

2kg	pork shoulder
500g	minced pork belly
500g	diced bacon
24	chopped sage leaves
4 tsp	thyme leaves
2 tsp	salt
2 tsp	cracked black pepper
2 tsp	ground white pepper
1 tsp	mace / nutmeg
1 tsp	cayenne pepper

Jelly

2	pigs' trotters
1	onion
1	carrot
1	stick of celery
10	black peppercorns
6	leaves of gelatin

Pastry

200g	lard *diced*
200g	butter *diced*
1.1kg	flour
3 tsp	salt
400ml	water
2	eggs *beaten*

For the Jelly (make 24 hours in advance)

Place the trotters into a deep pan with the roughly chopped onion, carrot, celery and peppercorns.
Cover with water and bring to the boil. Skim off any scum that forms on the surface.
Lower the heat and simmer for 1 hour, topping up with water as needed.
Strain the liquid and refrigerate overnight.
Remove the fat and place the jelly into a saucepan.
Bring to the boil, then allow to cool for 4 hours.
Strain off 500ml of liquid and add the gelatin, stir until dissolved.
Set aside.

For the Filling

Finely dice the pork shoulder.
Combine with the other pork pie filling ingredients.
Set aside.

Pie Case and Assembly

Warm the butter and lard in a pan until melted.
Place into a mixing bowl and allow to cool for 10 minutes.
Add the flour and salt and mix well.
Add the water to the mix to form a dough.
Rest for 1 hour.
Heat the oven to 180°C.
Line the bottom of a medium pie tin with ¾ of the pastry, setting aside ¼ for the lid.
Push the pastry up the sides of the tin, making sure there are no cracks.
Spoon in the pie filling mix.
Brush some beaten egg onto edges, then seal with pastry lid.
Make a small slit in the centre of the lid.
Cook for 30 minutes at 180°C and then cook for 1¼ hours at 160°C.
Remove from oven and glaze with beaten egg.
Cook for another 15 minutes.
Allow to cool.
Pour up to 500ml of stock through slit in lid, using a funnel.
Refrigerate overnight.

Smoked
EEL

"A light dish but full of flavour, using some of the best river produce that the region can provide."

STEAMED BIBURY TROUT
with Spinach, Mace & Smoked Eel

SERVES 4
PREP: 10 mins
COOKING: 10 mins

4	150g trout portions
4	large handfuls of spinach
½ tsp	mace
150g	diced smoked eel
100g	butter
	rock salt

Steam the trout for about 5 minutes until opaque.
Remove the skin and season with rock salt.
Heat half the butter and the spinach in a large pan, adding a pinch of salt and the mace.
Stir until almost wilted - this won't take long (a few minutes).
Add the eel and warm through.
Serve the eel and spinach on a plate.
Whisk the remaining butter into the spinach cooking liquor to make a sauce.
Place the trout on top of the spinach and then spoon on the sauce.

"This is a variation from a classic quiche using the best artisan cheese from my hometown."

SINGLE GLOUCESTER TART
with Onion

SERVES 8
PREP: 40 mins
COOKING: 1 hour
COOLING: 1 hour

For the Pastry

250g	pastry flour
150g	butter
1 tsp	icing sugar
1	egg yolk
3 tbsp	cold water
pinch of salt	

For the Filling

2	onions *sliced*
200g	single Gloucester cheese *diced into 1cm cubes*
1	bunch of chives *chopped*
1	bunch of spring onions *sliced*
300ml	double cream
4	free-range eggs
	salt and pepper
	splash of good-quality olive oil

For the Pastry

Mix together the flour and butter until it resembles breadcrumbs.
Add the icing sugar, salt, egg yolk and water.
Bring together to form a dough.
Roll pastry into a lightly-greased eight-inch tart case.
Chill in freezer for 20 minutes.
Preheat the oven to 160°C.
Lightly prick base of case, then cover with parchment and baking beans.
Bake tart case until lightly golden - about 10-15 minutes.
Remove from oven.

For the Filling

Reduce the oven heat to 120°C.
Cook the onions slowly in a saucepan with a splash of good-quality olive oil until caramelised.
Cover the bottom of the tart case with the caramelised onions and season.
Cover with sliced spring onions and the diced cheese.
Mix the cream and eggs and pour into the tart case.
Bake until the custard is set: roughly 30 minutes.
Remove from the oven and cover with chopped chives.
Leave to cool before serving.

"Although this dish uses a cheap cut of meat, the slow cooking process in the salt crust means it is packed full of flavour."

SALT BAKED PORK KNUCKLES
with Apple Sauce

SERVES 4
PREP: 30-40 mins
COOKING: 4½ hrs
COOLING: 45 mins

2 pork knuckles

For the Salt Dough
1kg plain flour
300g salt
3 egg whites
300ml water

For the Apple Sauce
4 Bramley apples *peeled, cored and sliced*
300ml water
100g sugar
juice of 1 lemon

For the Pork Knuckles
Preheat the oven to 150°C.
Mix the salt, flour and egg whites together in a bowl.
Add water and bring together as a dough - all of the water may not be needed.
Roll out the dough to a thickness of 1cm.
Encase the pork knuckles inside the dough.
Bake for 4½ hours and rest for 45 minutes.

For the Apple Sauce
Bring the water, sugar and lemon juice up to the boil.
Add the sliced apple and cook until soft.
Blend in the food processor and pass through a sieve.
Leave at room temperature.

Break the salt dough open and discard.

Serve the pork knuckles with the apple sauce.

FREE RANGE
EGGS £1·80 per Doz

STAUB
STAUB
STAUB
STAUB
STAUB
STAUB

"Lardy cakes are one of my fondest childhood food memories - from a time when proper artisan bakers were still around. There is nothing better than one of these straight from the oven."

GLOUCESTER LARDY CAKES
with Nutmeg

MAKES 6
PREP: 1 hour
COOKING: 25 mins
CHILL: Overnight

14g	dried yeast
85ml	warm full-fat milk
2 tsp	salt
475g	flour
6	large eggs
30g	sugar
340g	soft butter (plus extra for lining the ramekins)
½	freshly-grated nutmeg
250g	currants
300g	demerara sugar
250g	lard (plus extra for topping) *diced*

Stir the yeast, milk, salt, flour, eggs and sugar together.
Add the butter slowly until everything is combined.
Cover with cling film and leave to prove for 2 hours.
Knock back the dough and refrigerate overnight.
On a hard floured surface, roll the dough into a rectangle.
Scatter with the sugar, lard and currants, then grate the nutmeg over the top.
Roll up the dough to form a cylinder, the same diameter as your ramekins.
Cover with cling film and refrigerate for 1 hour.
Remove cling film and cut the dough into 5cm-thick slices to fit snugly into the buttered ramekins.
Add a little more lard and sugar on the top.
Cover with cling film again and leave to prove for 1-2 hours.
Preheat the oven to 190°C.
Bake for 25 minutes or until golden in colour.

HAYLAGE
FOR SALE
£5

"I've a firm belief that the South West is one of the best regions in Britain to be a chef. Its rich history of farming and food production and the range of high-quality produce is exceptional. Born and raised in Bristol, I'm proud to be a part of the city's (and surrounding area's) thriving culinary scene. It's an exciting time to be a chef in the South West."

"This is a fun dessert that we serve as part of our tasting menu and any flavour combination can be used. Here we have chosen elderflower, blackberry and raspberry, making a distinct late-summer fusion. The elderflower comes from a cordial, which we make in the spring - but shop-bought cordial is fine to use for the recipe."

ICED ROCKETS

Raspberry, Blackberry and Elderflower

MAKES 6 - 8
PREP : 15 mins
COOKING: 5-10 mins
FREEZING: 3-4 hrs, in stages

150g fresh raspberries
100ml water
50g sugar

150g blackberries
100ml water
50g sugar

150ml elderflower cordial
200ml water

Rocket lolly moulds

For the Raspberry purée
Place the raspberries, water and sugar into a small saucepan.
Bring to the boil.
Blend well to a purée.
Pass through a fine sieve to remove any seeds.

For the Blackberry purée
Place the blackberries, water and sugar into a small saucepan.
Bring to the boil.
Blend well to a purée.
Pass through a fine sieve to remove any seeds.

For the Elderflower
Mix the cordial with the water.
Add more cordial to taste.

Begin by filling one-third of the mould with the raspberry purée.
Freeze for an hour or until the purée is well frozen, otherwise it will bleed into the next layer.
Fill the mould up another third with the elderflower.
Place in the freezer.
After 45 minutes, remove and insert an ice lolly stick.
Push the stick so it just goes into the raspberry layer.
Return to the freezer.
When frozen, fill with blackberry purée.
Return to the freezer.

To remove from the mould, dip into a bowl of warm water for a few seconds, then gently pull out the lolly.

"Chowder is the quintessential American dish that is usually made with clams. Giving a British twist, the clams have been replaced with smoked haddock poached in milk and cream, which evokes childhood memories of cooking poached haddock in milk and parsley."

SMOKED HADDOCK *and Spring Vegetable Chowder*

SERVES 4-6
PREP : 45 mins
COOKING: 45 mins

700g	smoked haddock fillet *skinned*
3	banana shallots *finely diced*
1	clove of garlic *minced*
2	sticks of celery *finely diced*
½	white onion *peeled*
1	bay leaf
2	cloves
1 tsp	mild curry powder
2L	fish or vegetable stock
100ml	white wine
100g	butter
600ml	full fat milk
300ml	single cream
500g	Maris Piper potatoes *peeled*
100g	peas (frozen is fine)
100g	broad beans *skinned*
10	spears of asparagus *sliced*
100g	flat-leaf parsley *sliced*

For the Chowder Base
Sweat down the shallots, celery and garlic in the butter with the curry powder. Add the white wine and reduce by half, then add the fish stock and reduce by another two-thirds.

For the Haddock
Dice the potatoes into 1cm square pieces and wash them under cold water.
Blanch in salted water - ensure they still have a bite.
Refresh under cold water and drain well.
To cook the smoked haddock place the cream, milk, onion (studded with the cloves), bay leaf and garlic in a wide-based saucepan and bring to the boil.
Add the haddock and bring back to a slow simmer, then remove from heat and leave to steep for 10 minutes.
Remove the fish from the cooking milk and cream and return the milk and cream to a medium heat.

Into the chowder base, add the potatoes and bring back to a slow simmer, then add the peas, beans and asparagus.
Bring back to a slow simmer and flake in the smoked haddock.
Add half of the cooking milk and cream and bring back to a simmer.
Taste the potatoes and greens to ensure they are cooked.
Check the seasoning, adding more salt and pepper if needed.
Add the parsley and serve.

50'
50'
50'

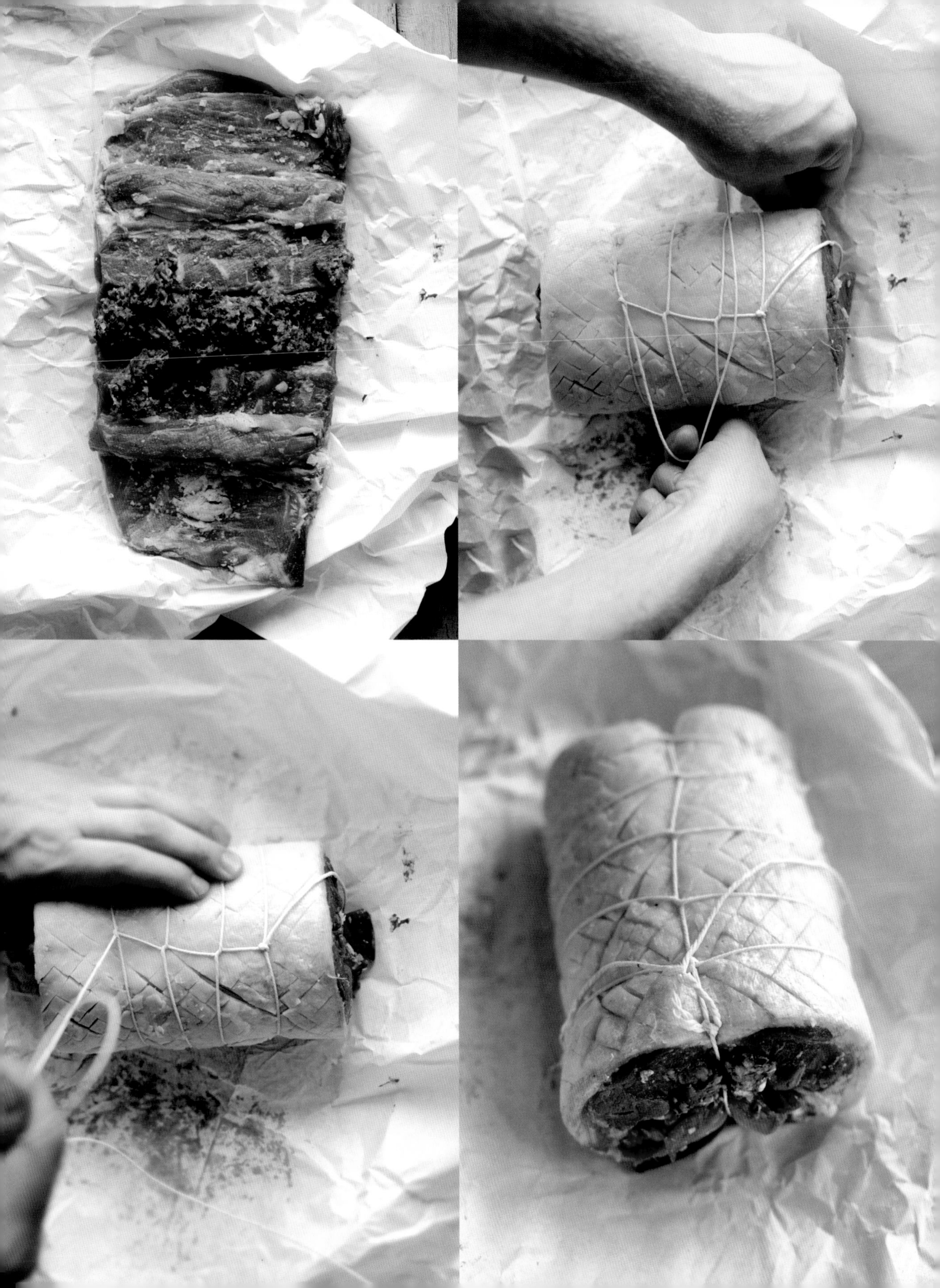

"This is ideal for any dinner party and can be prepared in advance. Once cooked, while you leave the lamb to rest for half an hour, you can relax and enjoy a drink with your guests."

STUFFED SADDLE *of West Country Lamb*

SERVES 6-8
PREP: 30-40 mins
COOKING: 45 mins
RESTING: 30 mins

1	saddle of lamb *boned out and trimmed of some, but not all of the fat*
8	cloves of garlic
8	sprigs of rosemary

For the Stuffing

200g	sausage meat
10	prunes *stoned*
200g	spinach *stalks removed*
25g	butter
1 pinch	freshly-grated nutmeg
50ml	port
30g	breadcrumbs
	salt and pepper to season

To make the Stuffing

Place the prunes into a small saucepan.
Add the port and bring up to the boil.
Remove from the heat and allow to cool.
Wash the spinach and pick off the stalks.
Heat the butter in a wide-based pan until foaming.
Add the spinach and nutmeg.
Remove from the heat and stir until the spinach has wilted.
Season with salt and pepper, then set aside until later.
When cool, chop the prunes and the spinach.
Add to the sausage meat with the bread crumbs.
Combine all the ingredients thoroughly and chill.

To prepare the Lamb

The fillets should be loose; remove them and set aside.
Score the fat both ways to form 1cm-sized diamonds.
Turn the saddle fat side down.
Place a cylinder of the stuffing in the middle of the joint.
Place the fillets on top, with the thick ends opposite each other.
Top with some more stuffing and season with salt and pepper.
Lift one of the ends and roll it over the loins.
Repeat this for the other side and ensure the joint is tightly rolled.
Tie with plenty of string so the joint holds its shape.
For cooking, season the outside.
Preheat the oven to 200°C.
Sear the joint all over in a large frying pan.
Transfer the joint to the roasting tin with the garlic and rosemary.
Roast in the preheated oven for 30 minutes.
Remove from the oven and cover with foil.
Leave to rest for 30 minutes - no less, as this is still part of the cooking process. The lamb should be medium to medium-rare.

"This dish was very popular in the late 1990s and has an amazing flavour, but you don't see it as much now. It is, however, a perfect winter warmer and a step up from the standard shepherd's pie."

LAMB SHANK
Shepherd's Pie

SERVES 6-8
PREP: 1 hour
COOKING: 4 hours

For the Braise

4	lamb shanks *about 350g-400g each*
2	carrots *peeled*
2	sticks of celery
2	medium white onions *peeled and split*
2	bay leaves
2	sprigs of thyme
1	bottle good-quality red wine
100g	tomato purée
1 tbsp	Worcestershire sauce
2	cloves of garlic *cracked*

For the Diced Vegetables

3	carrots *peeled*
2	medium white onions
2	sticks of celery
1	leek, white only
100g	butter

For the Mash

1kg	Maris Piper potatoes *peeled*
100g	butter
2	egg yolks

For the Braise

Preheat oven to 190°C.
Season the lamb shanks with salt and pepper.
Sear in a frying pan and colour all over.
Place the shanks in a large casserole dish or a deep roasting tin.
De-glaze the frying pan with a little of the red wine.
Place the onion, celery, carrot, garlic, bay and thyme in with the lamb shanks.
Cover with the red wine and top up with water or lamb stock.
Place on a lid and cook in the oven for about 3 hours or until the lamb is falling from the bone.
Remove from the cooking liquor and allow to cool a little.
Strain the cooking liquor through a sieve, place back on the heat and bring to the boil.
Skim off any fat or impurities and reduce down to about 400ml of liquid.
Shred the lamb off the bone - it should just fall apart.
Once the cooking liquor has reduced, add the tomato purée and Worcestershire sauce. Bring back to the boil - the liquor should coat the back of a spoon. Fold in the shredded lamb and the cooked diced vegetables.

For the Diced Vegetables

Dice the onion, carrot, leek and celery into 1½ cm squares.
Sweat down the onion, celery and carrot in the butter.
When the carrot is cooked to the bite, stir in the leek, take off the heat and leave to one side.

For the Mash

Peel the potatoes, wash and dice into 2cm squares.
Cook until just tender and strain.
Mash and add salt, white pepper, butter and the egg yolks.

To Finish

Place the lamb in a 2-inch-deep baking dish, level out and top with the mashed potato. Bake in the oven until the mash topping takes on colour and is starting to crisp.

"I love almond tart, and this tart takes advantage of the great British blackberry season. It is important to ensure the pastry is cooked well and has a lovely golden colour to guarantee a crisp finish."

BLACKBERRY TART
with Almond Frangipane

SERVES 6-8
PREP: 45 mins
COOKING: 1 hour
CHILL: 1½ hours

For the Pastry

220g	plain flour
100g	butter
100g	icing sugar
2	free-range eggs

For the Frangipane

125g	sugar
125g	butter
65g	plain flour
65g	ground almonds
3	free-range eggs *beaten*
30	blackberries
75g	blackberry jam

For the Pastry
Place all of the pastry ingredients into a food processor.
Blend until they come together. If a little dry, add a tablespoon of cold water.
Turn out and using hands, bring the pastry together - do not overwork it.
Shape into a disc, wrap tightly in cling film and place in the fridge to chill for 1 hour.
Preheat the oven to 180°C.
Roll out the pastry onto a lightly-floured cold work surface to 3mm thick.
Butter and flour a medium pastry case, then use the pastry to line the case.
Chill again for 30 minutes in the fridge.
Line the pastry case with baking paper and fill with dried beans or rice.
Blind bake in the oven for 15-20 minutes or until the pastry is golden and cooked through. Do not overcook or it will crack.
Remove from the oven and remove rice or beans carefully, and brush the hot pastry with egg wash - this will help to seal any small cracks.

For the Frangipane
In a mixer, cream the butter and sugar on a medium speed with a paddle.
This is the most important stage – it will take at least 15 minutes and the butter and sugar should double in volume.
Preheat oven to 140°C.
Add the eggs one by one - too much at once will make the mixture split.
If it does start to split, add a little of the weighed flour to bring it back together.
Once the eggs are incorporated, fold in the flour and ground almonds by hand.

Spread the jam on the bottom of the pastry case.
Fill with the frangipane mix and level out with a spoon.
Arrange the blackberries in circles. Do not push them in too firmly or they will be lost when the frangipane rises.
Bake for 30-40 minutes.

To test whether it is cooked correctly, insert a small knife in the middle - if it comes out clean then it is cooked; if a little is on the tip of the knife, bake for a further five minutes and test again.

FARM
SUITE
D &

TOM BLAKE

"I have cooking in my blood, having grown up on my mum's traditional home cooking and foraging – big Sunday roasts reinvented for Monday teas and lunch boxes crammed with banana and chocolate-chip cake. My first taste of a professional kitchen was a country pub, breaking down pheasants outdoors in the freezing cold, with nothing but two knives and a wonky chopping board. Now I bake, cure and make the most of cheap cuts and the very best of local, seasonal produce."

Fore
Rib
Sirloin
Thin
Rib
Flank

"This is a West Country version of the classic French rillettes. In this recipe I use a good-quality Somerset cider, which is great with the rich porky goodness. Using bacon cure on any pork, particularly slow-cooked pork, gives it a much deeper, well-seasoned flavour and the large quantity of fat makes it rich and spreadable. Try using pumpkin seeds in the winter when broad beans aren't available."

POTTED GLOUCESTER OLD SPOT *with Cider & Broad Beans*

SERVES 6
PREP: 45 mins
COOKING: 4 hrs
CHILL: 30 mins

500g	organic pork neck or trimmed shoulder *off the bone and rind removed*
500g	pork back fat *diced*
½	onion *roughly chopped*
2	sticks of celery *chopped*
½	bulb of garlic *roughly chopped*
2	sprigs of thyme, leaves only
4	juniper berries *crushed*
570ml	good-quality Somerset cider
100g	fresh English broad beans *podded and blanched*
	ground mace
	white pepper

For the Meat Cure

500g	fine sea salt
500g	demerara sugar
10	juniper berries
30	black peppercorns
5	bay leaves *chopped*

For the Meat Cure
Use a pestle and mortar to grind the peppercorns and juniper berries.
Combine with the other ingredients and store in a Kilner jar until needed.
(This cure can be used to flavour any pork. Try rubbing a handful over a pork belly before roasting. Leave for an hour, then rinse off with cold water and pat dry with a tea towel before it goes in the oven.)

Cover the pork meat and fat generously with a handful of bacon cure.
Leave in a plastic tub for 30 minutes.
Rinse off the cure from the meat and back fat.
Preheat oven to 150°C.
Place the meat, fat, chopped vegetables, juniper and thyme in an ovenproof dish.
Pour in the cider then cover with baking paper and tinfoil.
Make sure the seal around the edges is airtight or the pork will dry out and the cider will evaporate.
Cook in the oven for 4 hours.
Check the meat is tender and pulls apart easily.
Uncover and leave to cool for 30 minutes.
Blend the pork with all the liquid until smooth in a food processor.
Season with white pepper and ground mace - the bacon cure should have already provided enough salt.
Stir in the broad beans and divide into the pots.

Serve with piccalilli and good-quality wholemeal toast.

HERITAGE CARROTS

"This is a great variation on roast beef using a hugely understated cut. Brisket is from the belly of the animal and has all the quality of the very trendy pork belly. Like pork belly, it's cheap and flavoursome and should be cooked for a long time - and slowly."

SLOW ROASTED BRISKET
with Garlic, Fennel & Rosemary

SERVES 4
PREP: 15 mins plus 45 mins BBQ heating
COOKING: 3 hours

For the Brisket

1.2kg	organic beef brisket
2	sprigs of rosemary *chopped*
2 tsp	fennel seeds
6	cloves of garlic *grated*
1	onion *chopped*
2	sticks of celery *chopped*
1	carrot *chopped*
	flaked sea salt
	cracked black pepper
1	large glass of red wine

For the Dressing

1	bunch flat-leaf parsley *chopped*
1	clove of garlic *grated*
2 tbsp	capers *chopped*
1 tsp	English mustard
2 tbsp	olive oil
6	anchovy fillets *roughly chopped*

For the Brisket
Light the BBQ and leave to settle for 45 minutes before cooking.
Preheat the oven to 200°C.
Score the fat and rub the rosemary, garlic and fennel seeds all over the brisket.
When the BBQ is ready there should be no flames - just very hot red and white coals.
At this point, seal the beef on the BBQ.
Colour the beef all over - use large tongs as the fat from the beef will make the BBQ flame.
Put the beef on top of the chopped vegetables in a heavy-based roasting tray.
Place in the preheated oven for 15 minutes.
Take the beef out of the oven and pour in the red wine.
Turn the oven down to 150°C.
Cover the tray with baking paper and tinfoil to create an airtight seal - this will keep all the juices in to make a sauce.
Put the sealed tray back in the oven for 3 hours.

For the Dressing
Combine all of the prepared ingredients and drizzle over the sliced beef before serving.

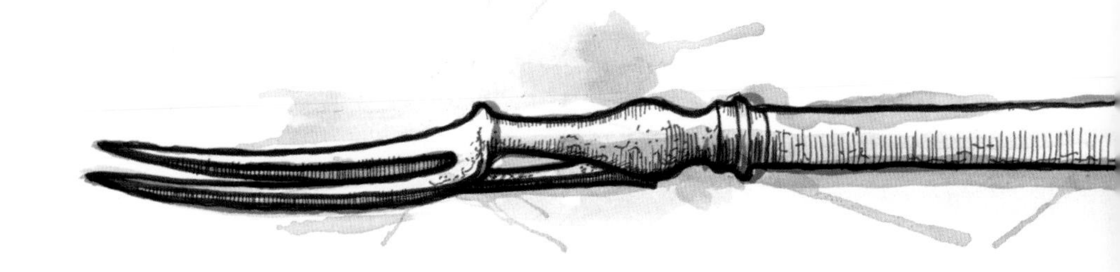

DAMSON PLUMS

"Light and refreshing, this baked custard is great with any sharp and tangy fruit. If you can't find any elderflower, use an extra vanilla pod in the custard. Real Somerset honey and vanilla help to take the edge off the fruits' acidity."

BAKED ELDERFLOWER CUSTARD
with Honey-Roasted Damsons

SERVES 4
PREP: 20 mins
COOKING: 1 hour

750ml	organic single cream
100g	caster sugar
9	organic egg yolks
1	vanilla pod
2	elderflower sprigs - washed
20	damson plums
2 tbsp	good-quality Somerset honey

Preheat the oven to 160°C.
Beat the egg yolks with the sugar until pale and creamy.
Slit the vanilla pod down the middle and scrape the seeds out with the back of a knife.
Put half in with the cream and set the other half aside for the damsons.
Heat the vanilla, cream and elderflower in a pan until just boiling.
Remove from the heat and slowly pour onto the egg and sugar.
Whisk thoroughly.
Butter a baking dish about 28cm x 20cm.
Pour the custard mix through a fine sieve into the baking dish.
Cook in a bain-marie with boiling water halfway up the side of the dish.
Cook until just set - it should just have a slight wobble. This should take 20-30 minutes.
Remove from the bain-marie and set aside to cool.
Wash the damsons.
Put them in a dish with the honey, remaining vanilla and 2 tbsp of water to stop the honey from burning.
Cook in the oven until soft.
When cool, push the stones out and serve with a generous helping of the baked custard.

"I changed from accountancy to become a fishmonger and now, as a self-taught chef, I remain a passionate supporter of the fishing industry. I'm proud of South Devon and genuinely believe in the quality of the seafood caught along the coast from Lyme Regis to Plymouth - it's the best in the world. "

"Red mullet is sensational, with a unique flavour and texture all of its own. When you fry the skin, it crisps wonderfully and has the flavour and smell of saffron and rich shellfish. The small flakes of flesh are moist and firm. A fish simply grilled whole with lemon is hard to beat, especially when done over a wood fire. This is my favourite fish."

GRILLED RED MULLET
with Lemon, Capers & Anchovies

SERVES 2
PREP: 5 mins
COOKING: up to 15 mins

2	whole red mullet weighing 300-350g *gutted and cleaned*
2	lemons *zest of 2 and juice of 1*
1	handful chopped parsley
1 tbsp	Dijon mustard
1 tsp	capers *roughly chopped*
1 tbsp	red onion *chopped*
4	cornichons *finely chopped*
5	anchovy fillets *chopped*
	extra virgin olive oil

Rub the mullet with olive oil and sea salt.
Preheat the grill or barbecue and grill either side for 4-5 minutes.

Alternatively, the fish can be roasted equally well with the oven preheated to maximum and the fish roasted for 10-15 minutes.

To make the sauce, combine the rest of the ingredients.
Season to taste and spoon over the cooked fish.

"This recipe is nearly always featured on the menu in my restaurant and it is a really popular choice. There is something wonderful about the fish arriving at the table in its bag. The flavours and aromas of heady rosemary and garlic being released as the little package is opened is all part of the pleasure. Make sure you use really fresh ingredients to produce a cracking result."

BAKED SEA BREAM *in Baking Paper*

SERVES 4
PREP: 10 mins
COOKING: 35 mins

1	sea bream weighing about 1.25kg *scaled and gutted*
4	sprigs of rosemary
1	small dried chilli
6	whole cloves of garlic
50ml	olive oil
½	glass dry white wine
1	lemon
	sea salt

Preheat oven to 200°C.
Place a piece of turkey-size tinfoil, about 70-80cm long, on to a work surface.
Cover with a layer of baking parchment.
Fold over each side so that the foil and parchment are secured together at the edges.
Put 2 sprigs of rosemary in the belly cavity of the fish and 2 in the centre of the parchment.
Lay the fish on the parchment and crumble the chilli over the top.
Lightly crush the garlic cloves by putting the flat side of a knife on top and giving them a thump.
Scatter them on and around the fish.
Sprinkle with sea salt.
Lift up the edges of the foil to keep everything in.
Add the olive oil and wine.
Encase the fish in the foil – it should be in a loose bag, but sealed tightly, enabling it to steam.
Place it on a roasting tray and bake in a hot oven for 35 minutes.
Remove from the oven and carefully undo the bag, folding back the sides to make the fish easily accessible.

Squeeze a little lemon over the top and serve.

"There's nothing quite like gorging on a plate of shellfish. Garlic is a perfect flavour with it, especially when mixed with rich melted butter and parsley. Use a selection of shellfish - the best you can find."

MIXED ROASTED SHELLFISH
with Garlic & Thyme

SERVES 4
PREP: 15 mins
COOKING: 12-13 mins

150g	butter
3	cloves of garlic
1	small handful of parsley *finely chopped*
	splash of Tabasco sauce
1	lobster, cut in half
2	scallops in the half shell
1	handful cleaned mussels
1	lemon
1	handful of clams
1	handful of shrimps
	a few sprigs of thyme
50ml	olive oil
1	small handful of breadcrumbs

Make the garlic butter by blending the butter, garlic and parsley in a food processor.
Season with salt and a little Tabasco.
Place a roasting tray over the heat, then add the olive oil and thyme.
When hot, add the lobster and shrimps and cook for 6-7 minutes.
Add the rest of the shellfish and breadcrumbs, and cook for a further 5-6 minutes, turning everything around with a large spoon.
Add the prepared garlic butter and let this melt.
Turn all the shellfish in the juices.

Add a squeeze of lemon and serve.

CARPET SHELL CLAMS

"Salty clam juice and sherry make a fantastic combination. The addition of a few sweet peas makes this a fine dish."

CARPET SHELL CLAMS
with Sherry & Peas

SERVES 4
PREP: 10 mins
COOKING: 10 mins

2	large handfuls of carpet shell clams
	olive oil
1	clove of garlic *crushed*
1 tbsp	parsley *chopped*
	dash of dry sherry
1	handful of peas *fresh, tinned or frozen*
	black pepper
	bread to serve

Wash the clams.
Heat some olive oil in a pan.
Add the crushed garlic clove and chopped parsley.
Add the clams, then a good dash of dry sherry.
As soon as the clams start to open, add the peas.
Wait for the clams to fully open.
Finish with plenty of black pepper.

Serve with fried or grilled bread to mop everything up.

"I started cooking at school in the fifth year for a laugh and ended up doing domestic science instead of metalwork. After school, I still didn't know what to do and when catering college was suggested, I just went for it. I feel very lucky living in the West Country, surrounded by first-class produce – a great deal of which ends up in my wood oven in Dorset; I love cooking this way and it makes for outdoor dining beyond compare."

"Seashore vegetables are a great natural accompaniment to fish and, if you are lucky enough to live by the seaside, you can pick them for free. Avoid buying pre-shucked scallops because they have usually been washed, which means they will have absorbed water."

HAND DIVED SCALLOPS
with Chorizo & Seashore Vegetables

SERVES: 4
PREP: 5 mins
COOKING: 7-8 mins

1 tbsp	olive oil
150g	chorizo
12	scallops *cleaned with shell*
60-80g	butter
	salt
	ground black pepper
	a handful of seashore vegetables such as sea purslane, sea beet and sea aster

Remove the skin from the chorizo.
Chop finely.
Heat the olive oil in a saucepan.
Cook the chorizo on a low heat for 4-5 minutes.
Break it up as it is cooking so it has the texture of coarse mince.
Heat some of the butter in a frying pan.
Season the scallops.
Cook the scallops upside down in the shells for about 1 minute.
Arrange the scallops on warmed serving plates.
Add the sea vegetables to the chorizo.
Heat for 30 seconds.
Spoon onto the scallops and serve.

RABBIT AND CRAYFISH
Stargazy Pie

SERVES 4
PREP: 1 hour
COOKING: 2½ hours

For the Rabbit

4	wild rabbits *back and front legs only*
	salt
	freshly-ground black pepper
3 tbsp	plain flour *plus extra for dusting*
3 tbsp	vegetable oil
2 tbsp	onions *finely chopped*
1	large knob of unsalted butter
150ml	English dry white wine or cider
2L	chicken stock

For the Crayfish

24	live freshwater crayfish
1 tsp	fennel seeds
12	black peppercorns
	few sprigs of thyme
2	star anise
1	bay leaf
1 tbsp	salt
1L	chicken stock

For the Pie

500g	good-quality puff pastry made with butter
1	beaten egg

For the Rabbit

Season the rabbit legs with salt and freshly-ground black pepper.
Dust them with one tablespoon of the flour.
Heat the oil in a heavy frying pan until hot.
Lightly brown the rabbit over a medium heat for 3-4 minutes on each side.
Remove and drain on kitchen paper.
In a large saucepan, gently fry the onions in the butter for 2-3 minutes until softened, but not coloured.
In a separate pan, heat the chicken stock to low simmer.
Dust with the remaining flour and stir well over a low heat for a minute.
Gradually add the wine and the hot stock, stirring to prevent lumps from forming.
Bring to the boil.
Add the rabbit legs and season lightly.
Cover with the lid and simmer gently for about one hour or until the rabbit is tender.
Remove the rabbit legs and leave to cool.
The sauce should be fairly thick - if it's not, continue simmering until it has reduced by half.

For the Crayfish

Put the fennel seeds, peppercorns, thyme, star anise, bay leaf and salt into a large saucepan of water.
Bring to the boil and simmer for 5 minutes.
Plunge the crayfish into the liquid.
Bring the water back to the boil quickly and simmer for 1½ minutes.
Drain and leave to cool.
Pick out four similar-sized crayfish for the garnish and set aside.
Peel the rest - including the large claws.
First remove the head and then squeeze the shell between thumb and forefinger to crack it. Set meat aside.

Crush the shells a little, put them in a saucepan with the chicken stock and simmer for 30 minutes.
Strain the stock through a sieve into a clean pan and boil to reduce to 4-5 tablespoons.
Mix the reduced stock into the rabbit sauce.

For the Pie
Once the rabbit legs are cool, remove the meat from the bones.
Mix the rabbit meat into the sauce with the crayfish meat.
Turn the mixture into a large pie dish or four individual dishes.
Preheat the oven to 200°C.
Roll out the pastry on a floured surface until about 3mm thick.
Using a sharp knife, cut out a lid that is about 2cm larger all round than the top of the pie dish - for individual dishes, cut the pastry into quarters, roll out and cut out four lids.
Brush the edge of the pastry lid with a little beaten egg.
Lay it on top of the dish, egg-washed side against the rim. Trim the edge and press down to seal.
Cut four small slits in the pastry lid - or a small slit in the centre of each of the individual ones.
Insert the whole crayfish, keeping the top half of the body above the pastry lid.
Brush the pastry with more beaten egg.
Bake the pie for 30-35 minutes or until the pastry is golden brown - small pies will take about 25 minutes.
Cover the crayfish with foil if they start to brown.

Serve with greens or mashed root vegetables such as celeriac or parsnip and small boiled potatoes with chopped herbs.

"Ask your butcher to save you some lamb fillets from under the saddle, which are perfect for a dish like this as they literally cook in a couple of minutes. If you can't get under-fillets then rump or loin will do just fine. The Portland is a small rare-breed sheep, once common all over Dorset, that takes its name from the Isle of Portland."

PORTLAND LAMB SALAD
with Scrumpy Fried Oysters

SERVES 4
PREP: 10-15 mins
plus 1 hour to rest batter
COOKING: a few minutes

For the Lamb
8 lamb under-fillets
2 handfuls of tasty salad leaves
ground black pepper
salt

For the Dressing
5 tbsp rapeseed oil
1 tbsp good-quality red wine vinegar *such as Cabernet Sauvignon*

For the Batter
150ml scrumpy or cider
100g gluten-free self-raising flour plus a little extra for dusting
4 medium rock oysters *shucked*

vegetable oil for deep-frying

Whisk the cider into the flour to form a fairly thick batter.
Leave to stand for 1 hour.

Preheat about 8cm of oil to 160-180°C in a large, heavy-based saucepan or electric deep-fat fryer.
Season the lamb fillets.
Heat a tablespoon of vegetable oil in a frying pan until almost smoking.
Fry the fillets for about 1 minute on each side.
Transfer to a plate to catch any juices.
Whisk the vinegar, oil and lamb juices together and season.
Put the salad leaves into a bowl and toss with half of the dressing, then arrange on four plates.
Slice the lamb thinly and arrange the slices on the salad.

Dip the oysters into the batter.
Drop them into the hot fat for a minute or so, turning them with a slotted spoon so they colour evenly.
When they are golden, remove them from the oil.
Drain on kitchen paper, then place on the salad.

"Matthew Fort made this dish on TV's Market Kitchen, so, as promised Matthew, I'm nicking the idea! I'm not sure where he 'borrowed' the idea from but it makes perfect sense to poach pears in their own alcohol, perry, and this makes a nice, simple, dinner-party dessert. You can simply serve this with thick cream, custard or ice cream."

POACHED PEARS *in Perry*

SERVES 4
PREP: 10 mins
COOKING: 1-1½ hours

500ml	perry
4	firm pears *peeled with the stalks left on*
4	cloves
1	small piece of cinnamon stick
6	black peppercorns
2 tbsp	caster sugar
4 tbsp	clotted cream *to serve*
1 cup	blackberries *crushed*

Put the pears, perry, spices and sugar in a saucepan.
Place a sheet of greaseproof paper on top of the fruit inside the pan.
Bring to the boil and simmer for about 45 minutes or until the pears are soft and tender but not falling apart.
Remove the greaseproof paper and the pears from the liquid.
Continue simmering the liquid until it has reduced by about two-thirds and thickened.
Return the pears to the liquid and leave to cool.
To serve, stand each pear on a deep serving plate.
Pour a few spoonfuls of the thickened liquid over each pear.

Serve with clotted cream and crushed blackberries.

NEIL HAYDOCK

"Having lived and worked in the South West since 2005, I now feel at home in a region that offers everything: a feast for the eyes with its rugged coastline, beaches and moorland, which are a joy to explore with Paula, my partner, and Bess our black Labrador. Bess provides animation to our walks by putting up pheasants and partridge, and by partaking in her favourite pastime - rock pool swimming - even in the depths of winter."

"Steamed puddings take me back to my Northern roots where a steak pudding can be found on every chip shop menu. This is my South West take on that traditional dish."

STEAMED LAMB PUDDING
with Stout

SERVES 4 - 6
PREP: 30-40 mins
COOKING: 3½ hrs plus cooling time

For the Suet Pastry

200g	beef suet
400g	self-raising flour
300ml	cold water
	salt

For the Lamb

800g	leg of lamb *diced*
3	medium onions *peeled and chopped*
2	medium carrots *peeled and chopped*
2 tbsp	flour
	vegetable oil
440ml	can of stout
2	bay leaves
2	sprigs of rosemary *picked and chopped*
	salt and pepper

For the Suet Pastry
Mix the flour with the suet and salt.
Add the water to bring the mix together into a dough.
Wrap in cling film and place in the fridge to rest.

For the Lamb
Preheat the oven to 180°C.
Peel and dice the onions and carrots.
In a large pan, sweat the carrots and onions with the vegetable oil.
When soft, add the lamb and herbs followed by the stout.
Stir in the flour and season with salt and pepper.
Add water – just enough to cover the meat – and bring to a simmer.
Put a lid on the pan and place in the oven for 2 hours, taking out to stir occasionally.
Remove from the oven and allow to cool.

For the Lamb Pudding
On a lightly-floured surface, take ¼ of the dough and roll it out to about 5mm thick for the lid.
Leave to one side.
Repeat the process with the remaining pastry.
Line a 1.75L greased pudding bowl with the pastry, leaving about a 1cm overhang.
Fill the basin with the lamb mix and brush the rim with water.
Place the pastry lid on top, remove the excess pastry and crimp the edges.
Cover with pleated foil to allow for expansion during cooking and secure the edge with string.
Place in a large saucepan and fill two-thirds of the way up the side of the pudding basin with boiling water.
Place a lid on the pan and steam for 90 minutes.
Remove from the pan, cut the string and remove the foil.

Serve with buttery mash and favourite greens.

"As the winter nights come upon us in Cornwall, the ocean teems with squid that come up from the deep to feed. Catching squid on jigs in the middle of a frosty night is a surreal experience for a chef, like me, who is more used to the familiarity and warmth of the kitchen. This dish is great served on grilled bread as a starter."

CORNISH SQUID
One Pot Wonder

SERVES 4
PREP: 15-20 mins
COOKING: 20 mins

600g	cleaned large squid *tubes and tentacles*
100ml	extra virgin olive oil
8	cloves of garlic *peeled and thinly sliced*
500g	cherry tomatoes *halved*
20g	marinated anchovies
100g	baby capers
1	small bunch of flat-leaf parsley
200ml	dry white wine

Slit down the length of the squid tubes and open them out.
Lightly score across the insides of the tubes making sure not to go the whole way through.
Turn the tubes and repeat to create a criss-cross pattern.
Cut each tube into quarters.

Heat the olive oil in a large saucepan and add the squid tubes and tentacles.
Add the rest of the ingredients.
Boil for 15-20 minutes on a high temperature, until the tomatoes have broken down, the sauce has thickened and the squid is tender.

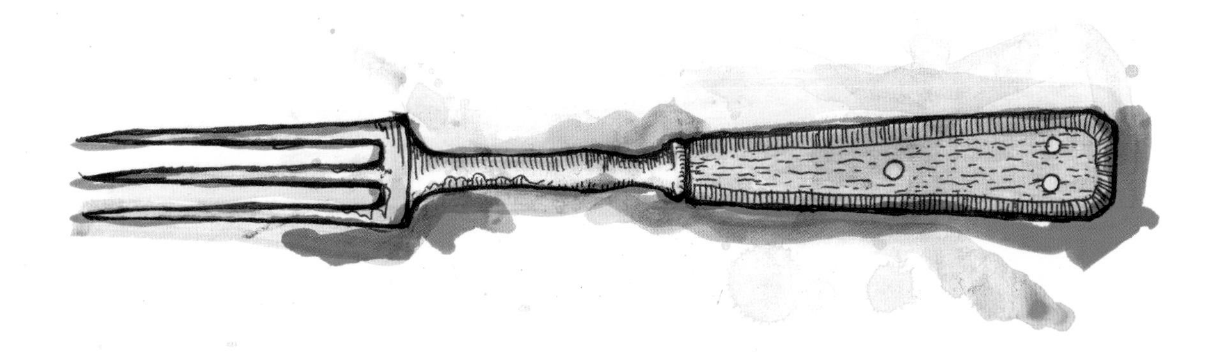

STAUB

STAUB

"Growing up with a grandfather who lived and breathed the countryside, rabbit on the table was as familiar to me as chicken is to most people. It was simply cooked in a pot for hours with carrots and onions, but that aroma and taste is, and always will be, unforgettable to me."

RABBIT PIE
with Cornish Ale

SERVES 4 - 6
PREP: 30 mins, plus 30 mins soaking
COOKING: 2 hours plus cooling time

1	rabbit *jointed*
1	carrot *peeled and diced*
1	onion *peeled and diced*
1	bay leaf
1	sprig of thyme
400ml	chicken stock
200ml	blonde beer
3	medium leeks *washed and finely sliced*
40g	butter
40g	flour
	salt and ground white pepper
250g	ready-rolled butter puff pastry
1	egg yolk

Soak the rabbit joints in cold water for 30 minutes to clean and whiten the flesh.
Drain the rabbit and place into a saucepan with the carrot, onion, bay leaf, thyme, chicken stock and beer.
Bring to a simmer and remove any scum.
Cook for about 1 hour - or until the rabbit is tender.
Drain the stock and set aside.
Preheat the oven to 180°C.
Take the rabbit pieces and place into a large pie dish, discarding the carrot, onion, bay leaf and thyme.
Bring the stock back to the boil and add the shredded leeks.
Cook until tender.
Mix the flour and butter into a paste and add to the stock.
Stir until the stock starts to thicken.
Reduce the heat and allow to simmer for about 2 minutes.
Season with salt and pepper.
Pour the sauce over the rabbit pieces.
Allow to cool before covering with the puff pastry.
Crimp the edges and brush with the egg yolk.
Place the pie in the oven for 20-25 minutes until a rich golden brown.

"Deer is a truly versatile, rich meat and low in cholesterol. There are shoulders for braising, legs for dicing, steaming or pot-roasting, and loin and fillet for pan-frying. The following recipe can be adapted for beef and also cooks well on a campfire."

VENISON STEW
with Potato Dumplings

SERVES 6
PREP: 30 mins
COOKING: 2½ hours

For the Venison

1kg	haunch of diced venison
4	carrots
	peeled and diced
3	medium onions
	peeled and diced
2	bay leaves
500ml	beef stock
250ml	red wine
2 tbsp	flour
	plus a little more for dusting
75ml	vegetable oil

For the Dumplings

3	large baking potatoes
2	egg yolks
	salt and ground white pepper

For the Venison
Preheat the oven to 180°C.
Heat the vegetable oil in a large ovenproof saucepan.
Add the carrots and onions and sweat for 2-3 minutes.
Add the venison and raise the heat to colour the meat lightly.
Add the red wine, stock, bay leaves and seasoning.
Stir in the flour and bring the stew to a simmer.
Place a lid on to the saucepan and place in the oven for 2 hours or until the meat is tender.

For the Dumplings
Prick the potatoes with a fork and microwave until cooked.
Allow them to cool slightly and peel.
Mash the potatoes in a bowl.
Season with salt and pepper.
Add the egg yolks and about a teaspoon of flour.
The mix should come together as a dry ball of potato - if it is a little wet, add another teaspoon of flour.
Divide the potato mixture into two and on a lightly-floured surface roll the potato into a sausage shape.
With a knife that has been dipped into flour, cut the potato sausage into 3cm lengths.
Repeat with the second ball of potato.
Place the dumplings on top of the venison stew.
Return to the oven, without a lid, for 10 minutes until the top of the dumplings are golden.

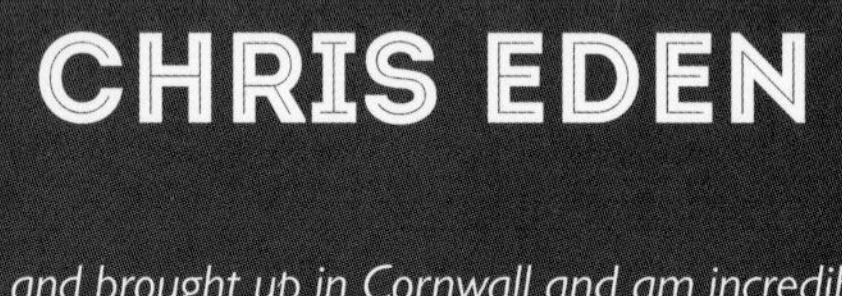

"I was born and brought up in Cornwall and am incredibly proud of my heritage. And a huge part of that is the food. I grew up eating my nan's packed lunches and watching her make pasties and saffron buns – I'm a proud Cornishman! The county is full of fabulous produce such as the Dexter beef that comes from a farm on the rugged south coast."

driftwoo

"To me, wild garlic signifies the beginning of spring and grows everywhere. Use hand dived scallops rather than dredged ones because dredging can damage the shells and they then require more thorough washing. As a result they absorb water which then seeps out during cooking."

HAND DIVED SCALLOPS
with Wild Garlic

SERVES 4
PREP: 5-10 mins
COOKING: 4 mins

4	half shell scallops
80g	wild garlic leaves
50g	toasted pine nuts
50g	grated Parmesan
	pinch of salt and pepper

Make sure the scallops are cleaned and free of dirt and grit.
Blanch the wild garlic in boiling water for 30 seconds.
Drain and refresh in ice-cold water.
When cool, place the wild garlic in a blender with the pine nuts, a pinch of salt and pepper and Parmesan, then blend for 1 minute to make a pesto.
Put the scallops (in their half shells) on a tray and place under a moderate preheated grill for 2 minutes.
Remove the tray from the grill and place a spoonful of pesto on top of the scallops.
Return to the grill for a further 2 minutes.

Serve with a wedge of lemon.

"This is a lovely harmonious dish with the root vegetables, plums and partridge all in season together. In Cornwall, partridge and pheasant are the main birds killed during shoots and are a great alternative to chicken and guineafowl. Partridge is easy to cook, and simple to portion - one bird per person."

PARTRIDGE WITH AUTUMN SLAW

Parsnip & Poached Plums

SERVES 4
PREP: 20-25 mins
COOKING: 45 mins

4	oven-ready partridges
1	parsnip

For the Slaw

2	carrots
2	beetroots
¼	Hispi cabbage
	shop-bought mayonnaise
	salt

For the Plums

4	plums
300ml	water
125g	sugar

For the Partridge
Preheat oven to 180°C.
Sear the partridges in a pan so all sides are golden brown.
Place in the oven for 12-15 minutes.
Remove from oven and allow to rest for at least 10 minutes.

For the Slaw
Slice the cabbage, beetroot and carrot finely.
Salt and leave for 10 minutes.
Wash the vegetables and place them in a dry cloth.
Pat dry and mix with the mayonnaise to make the slaw.

For the Plums
Bring the water and sugar up to the boil.
Cut the plums in half, remove the stone and place them in the hot liquid.
Bring back to the boil and cover with cling film.
Leave to one side: residual heat will continue to cook them.

For the Parsnip
Peel the parsnip into long strips, discarding the outer peel.
Cook in batches in a deep-fat fryer at 160°C until golden brown.

To serve, place all the components on a platter.

"The pasty is a traditional classic dish and for many is synonymous with the West Country. My mother made pasties for all the top chefs that I worked for and they loved them. This recipe is based on the one the miners used to take to work: a full meal in an easy-to-eat pastry parcel and as it makes its own gravy, no ketchup or brown sauce is required."

TRADITIONAL CORNISH PASTY
with Sweet and Savoury Filling

SERVES 4
PREP: 45 mins
CHILL: 30 mins
COOKING: 50 mins

For the Shortcrust Pastry

150g	lard
250g	plain flour
1	egg yolk
1 tbsp	milk
	salt

For the Filling

250g	beef skirt or chuck *diced*
1	potato *peeled and diced*
1	onion *diced*
½	leek *diced*
¼	swede *diced*
	salt and pepper
2	apples *peeled and diced*
	handful of raisins
	slice of white bread

For the Pastry
Dice the lard and gently rub together with the flour.
When it starts to come together add the salt, egg and milk.
Form to a smooth dough and leave in the fridge for at least half an hour before rolling.

For the Filling
Preheat the oven to 180°C.
Mix all of the savoury ingredients together.
Season well and leave in the bowl.
In a separate bowl, mix the apple and raisins and leave to one side.

For the Pasty
Remove the pastry from the fridge and roll to a thickness of about 2cm.
Cut into circles - size of circle according to preference.
Place the savoury filling on the left-hand side, up to the middle of the circle, leaving enough space to fold over.
Place a finger-sized piece of bread next to the savoury filling.
Place the apple and raisins on the right-hand side of the circle, making sure it is not loose.
Fold the pastry over to join the other side and crimp to seal the pasty.
Bake for about 50 minutes until golden.

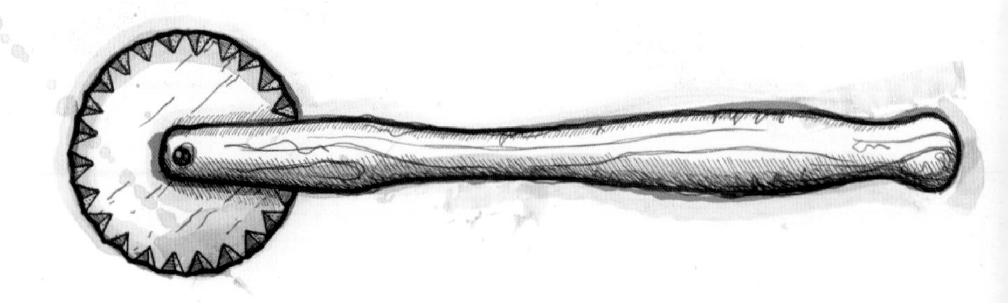

"The recipe makes more purée than is needed for this dish, but it freezes well and can be used again. Dexter beef comes from a farm that overlooks the ocean on the rugged south coast of Cornwall. The animals are a lot smaller than normal cows and are purely grass-fed, resulting in a beautiful texture and flavour."

DEXTER BEEF *with Mushroom Purée*

SERVES 4
PREP: 45 mins
COOKING: 4 hours for stock, 45 mins for cooking

For the Beef

500g	Dexter beef fillet
20	button onions or baby shallots
1	Hispi cabbage *chopped into quarters*

For the Mushroom Purée

1	onion *finely sliced*
300g	field mushrooms *finely chopped*
100g	unsalted butter
1	garlic clove
1	sprig of thyme
200g	whipping cream
125ml	mead

For the Red Wine Sauce

3kg	chopped chicken bones

If you can not get chicken bones, just use a good-quality chicken stock.

2	garlic cloves
2	sprigs of thyme
3	onions *finely sliced*
2	bottles of good red wine

For the Mushroom Powder

20g	a handfull of shop-bought dried mushrooms *blitzed to a powder*

For the Mushroom Purée

Sweat the onions in the butter until soft and without colour.
Add the mushrooms, garlic, thyme and seasoning.
Cook for 5 minutes until soft.
Add the mead and cook until reduced by half.
Add the cream and then reduce by half.
Blend into a fine purée.

For the Red Wine Sauce

Place the chicken bones, garlic and thyme in to a large pan and cover with water. Simmer for 4 hours.
Drain the stock and set aside.
Caramelise the onions in the pan and add the red wine.
Reduce by half.
Add the stock and reduce by half again. Strain the sauce and return to the pan. Reduce to the desired consistency.

For the Beef

Preheat the oven to 180°C.
Sear the beef in a pan and place in the oven. Cook according to preference - 15 minutes for rare, 20 minutes for medium or 25 minutes for well done.
Remove from the oven and rest for at least 10 minutes.
Place the shallots or button onions in a pan and sauté until golden brown.
Place in the oven for 5-10 minutes until cooked.
Place the cabbage quarters in a pan of salted boiling water and cook until tender.

To Serve

Place the purée lengthways across the plate.
Place the drained cabbage in the middle of the plate.
Slice the beef on top of the cabbage and arrange 5 shallots or button onions around each plate.
Pour the sauce over and around the beef and sprinkle with mushroom powder.

"This is a simple twist on the classic bread and butter pudding, and a real crowd-pleaser."

BREAD AND BUTTER PUDDING
with Blackberries

SERVES 4-6
PREP: 30 mins
RESTING: 30 mins
COOKING: 25-35 mins

For the Custard

150ml	semi skimmed milk
1	vanilla pod
2	large whole eggs
4	large egg yolks
100g	butter
50g	caster sugar
1	lemon - zest only
1	orange - zest only

For the Pudding

2	punnets of blackberries
12	slices of white bread
	softened butter to grease the baking dish
	demerara sugar for sprinkling

For the Custard
Warm the milk, butter, lemon zest and orange zest.
Split the vanilla pod and put both the pod and scraped seeds into the pan.
In a separate bowl, slowly whisk the eggs and egg yolks together.
Add the sugar.
Add the warm milk and leave to infuse and cool.

For the Pudding
Preheat the oven to 120°C.
Rub the softened butter around a baking dish and sprinkle with demerara sugar.
Cut the crusts off the sliced white bread.
Place a layer of bread in the dish.
Sprinkle some blackberries evenly along the layer of bread.
Alternate the layers using all of the bread and blackberries.
Strain the custard on top of the blackberries and sliced bread.
Leave to stand for 30 minutes, allowing the bread to soak up the custard.
Sprinkle with demerara sugar and place in the oven for 25-35 minutes until set.

Serve with cream, clotted cream or ice cream.

"Using curd is lovely, as it gives a wonderful acidic kick, followed by a rich, creamy flavour, and makes for a real flavour 'journey'. A versatile recipe, this is a unique accompaniment to both sweet and savoury dishes."

COWS' CURD
Ice Cream

SERVES 6
PREP: 15 mins
COOKING: 15-20 mins

300g	fresh cows' curd
150ml	semi-skimmed milk
5	egg yolks *from large eggs*
110g	white sugar

Place the milk and cows' curd in a pan and warm - do not allow to boil.
Whisk the egg yolks and sugar together and slowly add the warm milk mix.
Whisk together and return to the pan.
Heat gently whilst stirring for two minutes.

Chill and churn in an ice cream machine.

SIMON HULSTONE

"I have been cooking since my teens. After working my way through some of the top restaurants in Europe, I have now settled in Torquay with my wife, Katy, and three daughters. Bringing this extensive influence of traditional and world cuisine to the English Riviera, I am totally passionate about combining this influence with what I believe to be some of the best local produce in the UK. "

FEDERATION
2012

"Sometimes known as a West Country haggis, hog's pudding is a type of sausage produced in Devon and Cornwall. Containing pork and either oatmeal or pearl barley, it can be seasoned with cumin and black pepper and has a very distinct flavour and texture. Some variations exist in different areas with additions of leek and herbs, but all will work well for this recipe."

HOG'S PUDDING FRITTERS
with Grain Mustard Mayo

SERVES 4
PREP: 30 mins
COOKING: 5-10 mins

For the Choux Paste

50ml	water
50ml	milk
25g	butter
65g	plain flour
2	eggs

For the Fritter

250g	hog's pudding *skinned and mashed*
	salt and pepper
1 tsp	mustard seeds

Grain Mustard Mayo

100ml	home-made mayonnaise
1 tbsp	grain mustard

For the Choux Paste
Warm the butter, water and milk in a saucepan.
When the butter has melted, add the flour.
Stir and cook the mix until it comes away clean from the sides of the pan.
Transfer to a mixing bowl and beat in the eggs.
Keep beating until the mixture has cooled.
Season with salt and pepper.

For the Fritter
Heat a deep-fat fryer to 170°C.
Mix the hog's pudding, mustard seeds and choux paste together.
Add seasoning.
Spoon pieces into the fryer and cook until golden brown.
Drain onto kitchen paper and season lightly.

For the Grain Mustard Mayo
Combine the mayonnaise and mustard and serve in a bowl for dipping.

"Related to squid, cuttlefish is a favourite of southern Europe but is not so widely used here in the UK. Samphire (a kind of sea asparagus) and fennel are perfect accompaniments to the cuttlefish. Crunchy pork scratchings add texture and lift this dish to the next level."

CUTTLEFISH AND FENNEL SALAD
with Samphire & Pork Scratchings

SERVES 4
PREP: 60 mins plus freezing time
COOKING: 2-5 mins

2	medium-sized cuttlefish *cleaned, tubes only*
1	fennel bulb
1	lime
1	lemon
	rapeseed oil
250g	fresh samphire *washed*
1	packet of pork scratchings

Square the cuttlefish tubes off and lay them flat on top of each other.
Freeze until solid.
Use a meat slicer to thinly slice the cuttlefish to make shavings.
Alternatively, allow to defrost slightly and use a very sharp knife to cut as thinly as possible.
Slice the fennel into the finest strips possible.
Grate over the lemon and lime zest.
Add the juice of the lemon and lime, and marinate for 30 minutes.
Wash and blanch the samphire in salted water.
Heat a little oil in a non-stick pan.
When hot, quickly flash-fry the cuttlefish shavings – this should take a matter of seconds.
Add the samphire and the fennel and combine.
Remove from the heat and place into a serving dish.

To finish, add some chopped pork scratchings to give a lovely crunch and serve immediately.

"Serving raw shellfish to some people is a definite no-no, but scallops freshly caught and properly prepared are beautiful served raw. Here I have simply marinated them before serving in lime zest and juice. The addition of borage, with its lovely oyster and cucumber flavour, is wonderful. Pickled cucumber adds a tangy and fresh-tasting simple salad and works perfectly as a side dish at a BBQ."

MARINATED SCALLOPS
with Pickled Cucumber, Borage & Lime

SERVES 4 - 6
PREP: 30 mins plus 1 hour marinating

12	large scallops *out of the shell*
1	cucumber
50g	sea salt
1	lime
25ml	champagne vinegar
25g	white sugar
25ml	rapeseed oil
20g	borage shoots or flowers

Using a potato peeler, peel the cucumber from top to bottom making long strips.
Cover in the sea salt and leave for 10 minutes.
Rinse and pat dry.
Bring the sugar and vinegar to the boil.
Allow to cool, pour over the cucumber and marinate for 1 hour.
Slice each scallop into 4 discs and lay out on a tray.
Zest the lime and place both zest and juice over the scallops.
Marinate for 5 minutes and sprinkle with the oil.
Build up the ribbons of cucumber and scallops in a serving dish and garnish with the borage.

Pour over any remaining marinade and serve chilled.

"Fantastic wild mushrooms from the woodlands of Devon are always served on my menu when they are in season. Washed, dried and then roasted with smoked garlic and fresh cream, before serving on toasted sourdough bread, this dish is real autumn comfort food. If you really want to show off, add some hog's pudding or smoked bacon."

CREAMED WILD MUSHROOMS
with Smoked Garlic

SERVES 4
PREP: 15 mins
COOKING: 15 mins

300g	mixed wild and cultivated mushrooms (cepe, field, chestnut, girolle, button etc)
3	cloves smoked garlic *peeled*
200ml	double cream
2	shallots *peeled and sliced thinly*
30g	chopped parsley
4	slices of thick-sliced sourdough loaf
50g	unsalted butter
	salt and pepper to taste

Clean and cut the mushrooms into suitable sized pieces.
In a heavy-bottomed pan place the chopped smoked garlic, shallots and a small amount of butter and cook until soft.
Add the wild mushrooms and cook until golden.
Pour in the cream and reduce to a nice thick consistency.
Season to taste and keep warm.
Place the rest of the butter into a non-stick pan and heat until bubbling.
Add the bread and fry until golden and crispy, then drain off and keep warm.
Place toast onto plate and cover with the warmed mushroom mixture.

Sprinkle with parsley and serve immediately.

TANSY

"This dessert is a variation of a classic bread and butter pudding. Tansy is a wild herb which has beautiful yellow flowers and is a somewhat forgotten ingredient. It was very popular in the 18th century and, like most herbs, was used for medicinal purposes. This pudding recipe was given to me by my father and I have had great success with it in competitions - so much so, we named our first daughter Tansy."

TANSY PUDDING
with Ginger & Almond

SERVES 4
PREP: 20 mins
COOKING: 12-18 mins

50g	ground almonds
100g	caster sugar
50g	butter
425ml	double cream
3	eggs
½	Jamaican ginger cake *blitzed to a rough crumb*
	flaked almonds
4	sprigs of fresh tansy
100g	clotted cream

Preheat the oven to 150°C.
Bring the cream and butter to the boil.
Beat the eggs with the sugar.
Pour the double cream over the eggs and mix in quickly.
Pour the mixture over the crumbed ginger cake and ground almonds.
Place into buttered ramekins and garnish with flaked almonds.
Cook in a bain-marie for 12-18 minutes, until firm.
Remove from ramekins gently and serve with clotted cream and a sprig of fresh tansy.

Please note: Tansy eaten in large quatities can make you quite ill, and some people may be allergic. Eat the garnish at your own peril.

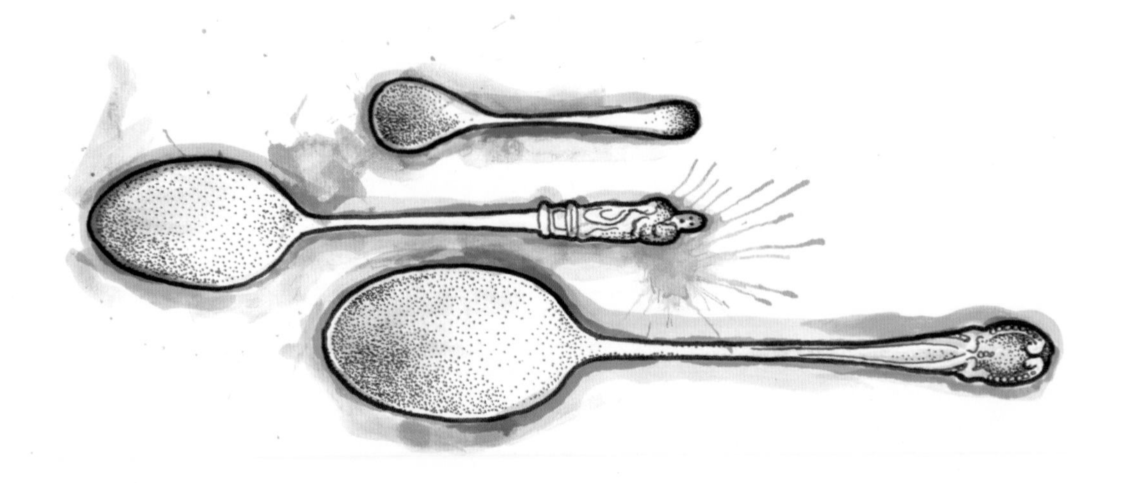

DARTMOOR

MICHAEL CAINES

"Growing up in a large family, we spent time around the table eating and in the garden growing fruit and vegetables - making extra pocket money by selling apples. I started baking with my mother from the age of 5 and gradually progressed to Sunday lunches. I have fond memories of the South West - crabbing in the rock pools, walking and camping, magical steam train rides, enjoying the sandy beaches and sailing. The West Country has a bounty of produce, making it one of the best larders in Europe - with its coastlines, lush pastures and high grazing lands."

"I love ham hock terrine, and here I've made mine with both smoked and green ham hocks. The smoky taste that you get from the mixture is lovely and using the cider to braise the hocks takes a traditional French classic and transforms it into a Devonshire celebration."

HAM HOCK TERRINE *with Cider*

SERVES 4
PREP: 30 mins, plus steep overnight
COOKING: 2-2½ hours
SETTING: 3-4 hours

2	ham hocks, ideally 1 smoked
2	440ml bottles of dry cider

For the Bouillon

1	large carrot *peeled and left whole*
1	onion *left whole and peeled studded with 3 cloves*
2	sticks of celery
1	small leek
1	bouquet garni
10g	black peppercorns
1	large sprig of thyme
1	large bay leaf

12g	leaf gelatin *soaked in water until soft*
75g	shallots
150ml	white wine
100ml	white wine vinegar

Soak the ham hocks in cider overnight.
The next day, place the ham hocks, cider and bouillon ingredients in a large pan and bring up to the boil.
Simmer gently for 2 hours until soft and allow to cool.
Remove and discard the studded onion.
Set the carrot, leek and celery aside.
Take out the ham hocks and trim off a little excess fat. Pull the meat apart into small chunks and set aside.
Drain the bouillon in a sieve and set aside to use as a setting agent later.

Place the shallots, white wine and white wine vinegar into a pan.
Reduce to a quarter of the original volume.
Add 1.5 litres of bouillon, bring to the boil and then simmer for 5 minutes.
Drain through a sieve, cool and add the soaked gelatin, stirring to dissolve.

Line a terrine mould with a double thickness of cling film.
Cut the carrot into quarters and thickly slice the celery.
Half-fill the mould with ham hock, then layer with the carrots, leeks and celery.
Finish filling the mould with ham, then add the ham hock jelly, to just cover the top of the ham.
Put in the fridge to set.
Once set, place a weight on the top to firm.

APPLE & BEETROOT JELLY
(great with a burger...)

SERVES 4
PREP: 30 mins
COOKING: 40 mins
RESTING: 3 hours straining time

500g	Bramley apples *peeled and chopped*
250g	Cox apples *peeled and chopped*
250g	beetroot *peeled and chopped*
250g	caster sugar
750ml	water
5g	pectin
20ml	apple vinegar
1	lemon *juice only*

Place the apples and beetroot into a thick-bottomed stainless steel pan.
Add the lemon juice, apple vinegar, sugar and water.
Bring to the boil and reduce to a simmer.
Simmer for 40 minutes, until the apples are cooked.

Line a colander with a muslin cloth and place over a pan.
Place the apple mixture in the muslin cloth and tie into a bag.
Hang the muslin 'bag' and leave to drain for 3 hours.
Add the pectin, then bring the drained liquid back to the boil.
Skim away any scum from the top and then reduce to 500ml.
Pour into jars and leave to cool.

Top with lids and then steam the jars for 30 minutes to sterilise them.

"I love making burgers with the children. Prime minced beef mixed with herbs and onions creates a full-flavoured burger that is delicious served with gooseberry relish. Gooseberries make great chutney: naturally acidic and delicious when blended with onion and grain mustard."

DEVON RUBY RED BURGERS
with Gooseberry & Mustard Relish

SERVES 6 - 8
PREP: Make relish a few days ahead of cooking burgers
COOKING: 30 mins

For the Relish

100g	onions *peeled and chopped*
30ml	olive oil
2	cloves garlic *crushed*
1	sprig of thyme *leaves only*
½	bay leaf
60ml	white wine vinegar
30g	grain mustard
200g	gooseberries *whole*
25g	sugar
½ tsp	pepper
½ tsp	ground coriander

For the Burgers

600g	minced beef
100g	onions *peeled and chopped*
60g	wholegrain mustard
10g	butter
10g	thyme *finely chopped*
10g	parsley *finely chopped*
15g	chives *finely chopped*
5	cloves of garlic *crushed*
2	eggs
10g	white breadcrumbs
	a little olive oil
	a little salt
	white ground pepper

For the Relish

In a pan, sweat the onions and crushed garlic in olive oil without colouring.
Add a pinch of salt and the herbs.
Add the white wine vinegar and reduce by two-thirds.
Add the grain mustard and reduce further.
Add gooseberries, sugar, pepper and coriander and cook for 30-45 minutes or until a thick consistency is achieved.
Season and leave to cool.
Mix together well and check seasoning.
Store for at least 2 days before using.

For the Burgers

Heat the olive oil in a pan.
Cook the onions on a medium heat until soft and transparent.
Place in a bowl along with all of the other ingredients and mix well.
Leave to rest in the fridge for 1 hour.
Shape into burgers and place onto a slightly oiled tray.

Grill, oven-roast or pan-fry the beefburgers according to preference and serve.

"Taking the humble cauliflower and pairing it with Brixham scallops makes this a celebration of texture and flavour. The firm, roasted scallops contrast with the cauliflower purée which, because it has been caramelised, intensifies the flavour and gives it even greater depth."

PAN FRIED BRIXHAM SCALLOPS
with Caramelised Cauliflower Purée

SERVES 4
PREP: 15-20 mins
COOKING: 35 mins

For the Cauliflower Purée

2	large cauliflowers
50g	unsalted butter
	water
	salt
	ground black pepper

For the Scallops

8	large Brixham scallops
	olive oil
	lemon juice
	salt
	ground black pepper

For the Cauliflower Purée
Remove the green leaves from the cauliflower and cut into medium-sized florets.
Put the florets in a saucepan, cover with water and bring to the boil.
Simmer until the florets are completely cooked through.
Using a colander, strain the cauliflower over a bowl and retain the cooking water.
Blend the cauliflower into a fine purée.
Melt 25g of butter in a large non-stick pan.
Put half of the cauliflower purée into the pan and start to caramelise, whisking occasionally.
Once the mixture has browned, set aside and repeat with the other half of the purée.
Blend the browned cauliflower purée once more.
Adjust the texture with a little cooking water.
Season to taste with salt and pepper.

For the Scallops
Season the scallops with salt and pepper on both sides.
Heat some olive oil in a non-stick pan and place the scallops in the hot oil.
Pan-fry the scallops for 2 minutes then turn them over and continue to cook for a further 2 minutes, taking care not to overcook them.
Squeeze some lemon juice over the scallops before serving.

To Serve
Spread some cauliflower purée into the middle of the plate and then place the scallops on top.

COD

ROASTED BRIXHAM COD
with Creamed Leeks & Wild Mushrooms

SERVES 4
PREP: 20 mins
COOKING: 20-30 mins

For the Fish

1	large fillet of cod *skinned and lightly salted*
100g	mixed wild mushrooms
1	leek
100ml	single cream
100g	fresh spinach

For the Sauce

15g	butter
40g	sliced shallots
100g	sliced button mushrooms
125ml	fish stock
125ml	dry white wine
20g	chives
	a dash of single cream
	unsalted butter
	a squeeze of lemon

For the Sauce

In a pan, sweat the sliced shallots in the butter until soft, but do not colour.
Add the sliced button mushrooms and sweat for a further 2 minutes.
Add the white wine and reduce by half.
Add the fish stock and reduce by one-third.
Add a dash of cream and whisk in some unsalted butter.
Season with salt, pepper and a squeeze of lemon juice.
Pass through a fine sieve.

For the Fish

Preheat oven to 200°C.
Cut the cod into 4 portions.
Chop the leek and mushrooms and wash the spinach.
Cook all separately in butter, adding a little reduced cream to the leek.
Season the cod with pepper and pan-roast for 10 minutes in olive oil.
Add a little butter towards the end of cooking.
Remove from the pan and add a few drops of fresh lemon juice.

To Serve

Spoon the creamed leek into the centre of the plate and place the cod on top.
Put the mushrooms and spinach garnish around the fish.
Add chopped chives to the sauce and spoon over the fish.

"I love this cider and fruit jelly summer recipe. Children are not the only ones who love jelly and ice cream, but this one is definitely for the grown-ups!"

SPARKLING CIDER JELLY
with Blackberries & Apple Cider Ice Cream

SERVES 4
PREP: 30-40 mins
COOKING: 30 mins
CHILLING: 2-3 hours

For the Cider Jelly

4	leaves of gelatine
500ml	sparkling cider
60g	caster sugar
125g	blackberries *fresh or frozen*

For the Apple Compote

750g	Granny Smith apples *peeled and chopped*
100g	butter
100g	sugar
1	vanilla pod *slit and scraped*

For the Apple Cider Ice Cream

500ml	milk
25g	milk powder
4	egg yolks
50g	sugar
100ml	cream
20ml	Somerset cider brandy
100g	apple compote *(see above)*
1L	cider, reduced to 100ml

For the Cider Jelly
Soak the gelatine leaves in cold water until soft.
In a separate pan, bring 100ml of cider to the boil and stir in the sugar until dissolved.
Add the berries and lightly poach.
Remove the berries from the liquid and divide into the moulds.
Stir the softened gelatine into the pan and add the remaining cider.
Stir and then pour into the moulds.
Chill for an hour or so until set.

For the Apple Compote
Put the butter in a stainless steel saucepan over a low heat.
As soon as it starts to melt, add the apples, sugar and vanilla pod.
Cook the apple to a compote stirring from time to time.
If the texture is too thin, leave to reduce down until the compote thickens.
Remove the vanilla pod, scraping it again first.
Blend the apple compote to a fine pulp and pass through a fine sieve.
Place in a container and reserve for later use.

For the Apple Cider Ice Cream
Cream together the sugar and egg yolks in a bowl.
In a saucepan, bring the milk, cream and milk powder to the boil.
Pour some of the milk onto the sugar and egg yolks and mix together.
Return the mixture to the saucepan and cook to 85°C.
Allow to cool and then stir in the apple compote, cider brandy and cider reduction.
Transfer to an ice cream machine and freeze.

To Serve
Turn the jellies out onto individual plates and sit a scoop of the apple cider ice cream with each one.

DUCK
EGGS

RECIPES
(in some kind of order...)

SOUP AND SNACKS

FISH

SHELLFISH

LAMB

PORK

BEEF

POULTRY AND GAME

BAKING AND PUDDINGS

RESTAURANTS
and Contact Details

NATHAN OUTLAW
Restaurant Nathan Outlaw
St Enodoc Hotel
Rock
Cornwall
PL27 6LA
01208 862 737
mail@nathan-outlaw.com
www.nathan-outlaw.com
See also:
www.outlaws.co.uk
www.capitalhotel.co.uk
www.academynathanoutlaw.com

PETE BIGGS
The Capital Hotel
22-24 Basil Street
Knightsbridge
London
SW3 1AT
020 7589 5171
reservations@capitalhotel.co.uk
www.capitalhotel.co.uk

PAUL AINSWORTH
Number 6
6 Middle Street
Padstow
Cornwall
PL28 8AP
01841 532 093
enquiries@number6inpadstow.co.uk
www.number6inpadstow.co.uk
See also:
www.paul-ainsworth.co.uk
www.rojanos.co.uk

JACK STEIN
The Seafood Restaurant
Riverside
Padstow
Cornwall
PL28 8BY
01841 532 700
reservations@rickstein.com
www.rickstein.com
See also:
www.rickstein.com/developmentkitchenblog

SAM MOODY
The Bath Priory Hotel
Weston Road
Bath
BA1 2XT
01225 331 922
mail@thebathpriory.co.uk
www.thebathpriory.co.uk
See also:
www.brownswordhotels.co.uk

RUSSELL BROWN
Sienna Restaurant
36 High West Street
Dorchester
Dorset
DT1 1UP
01305 250022
browns@siennarestaurant.co.uk
www.siennarestaurant.co.uk
See also:
www.chefrussellbrown.co.uk

TANNER BROTHERS

Tanners Restaurant
Prysten House
Finewell Street
Plymouth
PL1 2AE
01752 252 001
enquiries@tannersrestaurant.com
www.tannersrestaurant.com
See also:
www.barbicankitchen.com

MICK SMITH

Porthminster Restaurant
Porthminster Beach
St Ives
Cornwall
TR26 2EB
01736 795 352
info@porthminstercafe.co.uk
www.porthminstercafe.co.uk

TOM KERRIDGE

The Hand and Flowers
126 West Street
Marlow
SL7 2BP
01628 482 277
reservations@thehandandflowers.co.uk
www.thehandandflowers.co.uk

JOSH EGGLETON

The Pony and Trap
Newtown
Chew Magna
Bristol
BS40 8TQ
01275 332627
info@theponyandtrap.co.uk
www.theponyandtrap.co.uk

TOM BLAKE

The Swan Wedmore
Cheddar Road
Wedmore
Somerset
BS28 4EQ
01934 710 337
info@theswanwedmore.com
www.theswanwedmore.com

MITCH TONKS

The Seahorse
5 South Embankment
Dartmouth
TQ6 9BH
enquiries@seahorserestaurant.co.uk
www.seahorserestaurant.co.uk
See also:
www.mitchtonks.co.uk
www.rockfishgrill.co.uk

MARK HIX

Hix
66-70 Brewer Street
London
W1F 9UP
020 7292 3518
www.hixsoho.co.uk
See also:
www.hixoysterandchophouse.co.uk
www.hixoysterandfishhouse.co.uk
www.marksbar.co.uk
www.hixatselfridges.co.uk
www.thealbemarlerestaurant.com
www.chickenandsteak.co.uk

NEIL HAYDOCK

Watergate Bay Hotel
Watergate Bay
Cornwall
TR8 4AA
01637 860543
life@watergatebay.co.uk
www.watergatebay.co.uk

CHRIS EDEN

Driftwood Hotel
Rosevine
Portscatho
Cornwall
TR2 5EW
01872 580644
info@driftwoodhotel.co.uk
www.driftwoodhotel.co.uk

SIMON HULSTONE

The Elephant Restaurant
3 & 4 Beacon Terrace
Torquay
Devon
TQ1 2BH
01803 200 044
info@elephantrestaurant.co.uk
www.elephantrestaurant.co.uk

MICHAEL CAINES

Gidleigh Park
Chagford
Devon
TQ13 8HH
01647 432 367
gidleighpark@gidleigh.co.uk
www.gidleigh.com
See also:
www.michaelcaines.com
www.abodehotels.co.uk
www.brownswordhotels.co.uk

This book is the product of much work by many people.

Of everyone involved, the most thanks must go to my wife, Maria, the most patient person I know. Thanks for listening to me talk incessantly about every detail and idea at length for the last nine months. Your patience, feedback and help have formed this book into something we can both be proud to have completed. You are the best. Thanks also to our two little monkeys Charlie and Jack, the most astonishing sons a dad could wish for - thanks for testing out some of the baking recipes; love you guys. xxx

Without the chefs this would be just a picture book. Thank you for the generosity with your time, produce and recipes. I really do respect how hard you guys work and how precious time is to you - thanks for giving up some of it to get involved in the book. Much respect.

A massive thank you to the lovely Jane Griffiths - for putting in the hours with your keen eye. Thanks for your attention to detail and for correcting all of the creative ways we were using words... Merci, gracias, much obliged! x

A big cheers also to the very talented Becky Ritson for helping out with the additional copy – you have got some super skills.

Thanks also to Portia Spooner for proofreading through the recipes; you are always a pleasure to work with and I can't wait to shoot in the new kitchen!

Love and thanks to Louise Cole, Abigail Bruce and Rosie Smith for helping out in the final stages, greatly appreciated!

Thanks also to Michelle Simms, Michael Walsh and Katie Johns for talking through the visual ideas at the start.

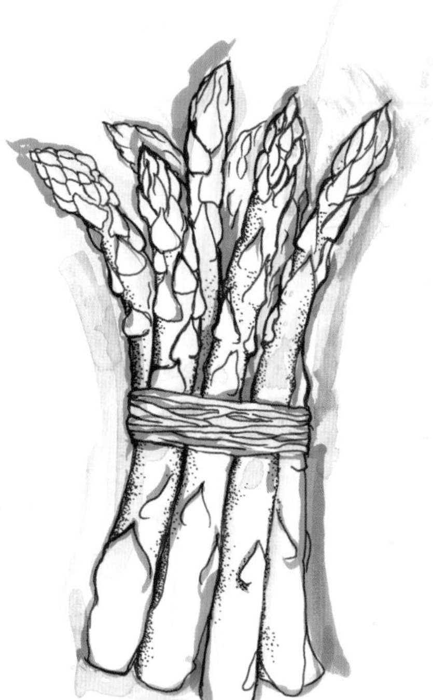

A special thanks to the following Estates and Producers:

Prideaux Place – for your help rounding up some very flighty deer.
www.prideauxplace.co.uk

Brown and Forest - for showing me how you smoke your eel.
www.smokedeel.co.uk

Bibury Trout Farm – for fishing out a beautiful fresh trout for me to photograph.
www.biburytroutfarm.co.uk

Deli Farm Charcuterie – for letting me photograph some of your tasty meat in the wood shed.
www.delifarmcharcuterie.co.uk

Penare Farms – for taking me on a muddy walk to photograph the cattle on the cliff tops.
www.penarefarms.co.uk

Cheddar Gorge Caves – for allowing me access to the precious cheese.
www.cheddargorge.co.uk

Fresh from the Sea – for taking me out fishing Calum, I have total respect for how hard fishermen work as a result (sorry about the sick).
www.freshfromthesea.co.uk

Food and lifestyle photographer David Griffen loves food almost as much as he loves photography. He relocated from Australia to Cornwall nine years ago and now lives and works here with his young family.

David regularly shoots for the top echelon of chefs in the region and further afield, including Nathan Outlaw, Paul Ainsworth and Tom Aikens, and has just finished shooting Michael Caines' first cook book.

David actively engages with a steadily growing audience through various social media channels, and is a leading expert in the fields of 'photography for food blogs' and 'food photography for social media promotion'.

www.davidgriffen.co.uk

RESPONSIBLE
FISHING SCHEME